WE FOUGHT THEM ON THE SEAS
Seven Years in the Royal Navy

A Memoir by
Lieut. Ian S. Menzies, D.S.C. R.N.V.R.

Illustrations by Barbara Newton Menzies

WE FOUGHT THEM ON THE SEAS
Seven Years In The Royal Navy
Ian Menzies

Published by
The Cheshire Press
52 Main Street
North Reading, MA 01864
www.cheshirepress.com

ISBN: 978-0-9853689-5-1

Library of Congress Control Number: 2012953295

Printed in the United States of America

Menzies, Ian
WE FOUGHT THEM ON THE SEAS: Seven Years In The Royal Navy

Ilustrations by Barbara Newton Menzies

DEDICATION AND ACKNOWLEDGMENTS

This book, centered on seven years of war
in the Royal Navy in World War 2,
is dedicated to my parents,
John Stewart Menzies and Gertrude A. Mephius,
to whom I owe everything, and to my loving wife of 60 years, Barbara
(Newton) Menzies

★

This book is also a gift to my children,
Marla, Gillian, Alexa and Deborah
and also to my grandchildren,
Skye Cohan and Caitlin (Cohan) Gibson
and to my great-grandchildren, Nikolaus and Elisette Gibson
and their father Albert Gibson

★

It is furthermore left with loving memories
to my loyal companion of many years
Claire Nelson Davies

★

And in acknowledgment, I wish to thank those who pushed and
cajoled me to revive and complete a 53-year-old draft of the book:
Professors Robert C. Wood and Irving H. Bartlett and most
forcefully James M. Coull, Leonard E. Lynch
and my son-in-law John A. Cohan.
My thanks to them all and to a family team of typists, computerites,
researchers and advisers including
Marla, Deborah and Gillian Menzies.

★

Finally it is in memory and tribute to all those who made the ultimate
sacrifice for freedom as well as those, civil and military, who suffered
grievous wounds and disabilities. We, who somehow survived, do not
forget them. Nor should you.
They assured our freedom at enormous cost.

We shall not flag or fail. We shall go on to the end. We shall fight in France, we shall fight on the seas and oceans, we shall fight with growing confidence and growing strength in the air, we shall defend our island, whatever the cost may be, we shall fight on the beaches, we shall fight on the landing grounds, we shall fight in the fields and in the streets, we shall fight in the hills, we shall never surrender.

Winston Churchill
Speech on Dunkirk, House of Commons,
June 4, 1940

CONTENTS

FOREWORD

There will be readers who will ask, not unreasonably, how can he remember events in such detail, personal detail, during almost seven years of World War II in the Royal Navy in three different destroyers as well as other ships, in theatres from the North Sea to the North Atlantic, from the English Channel to the Mediterranean and from the West Indies to West Africa and the South Atlantic.

Two reasons. I kept diaries during the war years; a practice I readily admit is frowned upon by the Royal Navy, although I did keep them in a manner that would not disclose technical or tactical information. Also, I completed an entire draft of my war years immediately after demobilization.

I contacted one publisher who was inundated with war books and who made some suggestions that I couldn't meet as one newly married, changing countries and seeking employment.

So the typewritten pages went into a bottom drawer and stayed there for some 60 years, except for an occasional withdrawal to supply a fact or two for a newspaper article or speech.

The miracle is that both paper and typewriter ribbon stood up to the passage of time.

Through those years, despite the urgings of family and friends to produce a book, I held off, perhaps fearing the task of revision too much for a retiree, and a nonagenarian at that.

But then I realized, watching great-grandchildren at play, that I, in fact, did owe my family something, and that I could turn the story of a young man's coming of age in a war—a never-to-be-forgotten summit of his life—into an autobiography, something those that follow might ponder.

All I needed to do was enlarge the beginning—tell a little more about the author—and bring the war story to a civilian conclusion. And that's what I have endeavored to do.

CHAPTER ONE

Journalism An Alternative

The small boy of eight was engrossed in the film. Suddenly, unable to contain himself a minute longer, he shouted, "Come on the Scotch Navy!" The theatregoers around him smiled. His mother admonished him—not sharply, but laughingly. His eyes were bright, his expression tense as he watched the coal-begrimed husky stokers feeding the ever-hungry cruiser's furnaces. They were burning even the officers' piano in an effort to increase the flaming power of this large cruiser of the Royal Navy and to coax out one more knot of speed.

It was the "Battle of the Falkland Islands" re-enacted on the screen—the historic chase of a vaunted German raider squadron by the Royal Navy in World War I in the southern latitudes off Cape Horn—a battle of revenge and long-seeking. The little lad was watching it draw to its conclusion as first one German raider and then another was overhauled and left a sinking, burning shambles. Honor was satisfied and so was he.

Born in 1920 after the war to end all wars, and of limited-income, middle class parents, I was brought up as a single child in an atmosphere of what I would like to call "averageness."

Ian Menzies as a boy 8 years of age.

The years following World War I were difficult the world over. The social problems of unemployment, expensive housing, inflation and the many difficulties we know so well, reflected the general difficulties of the times. My life, however, was relatively untroubled by the impact of these social disturbances and though unable to realize any luxuries, I was denied no essentials. I was blessed with caring, thoughtful parents.

My home, a flat, was in Scotland's largest city, industrial Glasgow, in my day infamous for its slums and razor gangs and famous for its ships—*The Queen Mary* and the first *Queen Elizabeth*. Glasgow was tough, but an exciting city, and at root, a friendly city. Edinburgh was and is the capital, a bit snobby and distant but Scotland's showpiece.

I attended one of Glasgow's many Scottish-type day schools which charged varying fees. They were, to be honest, a "step-up" socially and educationally from the city's then public schools—free schools, not the public schools of the high cost English type public boarding schools.

Scotland has a built-in historic reverence for education, as shown by the attainments of many of its sons and daughters—doctors, engineers, scientists, writers, explorers, architects and so on. But sometimes I wonder how and why, when I think of the classes I attended—classes of 50 students in the elementary grades and 30 in the upper grades—how could a teacher possibly handle the numbers?

Was corporal punishment a natural outcome of this burden? I know not. But in my day I know it was in vogue. I cannot recall a single teacher above the early elementary grades who did not resort to using a strap or a belt in a final endeavor to maintain discipline or punish laziness or failure to do homework.

I cannot frankly say I enjoyed school, being only an average student. My interest was more into sports than classical studies, although I loved history, geography, literature and books of all kinds; in this, I was encouraged by my mother, a great reader herself, who wrote some award-winning poetry.

My father, as fathers do, fed my sports enthusiasm and got me involved in the scout movement which, in turn led to cycling, camping, yachting and hill climbing, and eventually even to trips abroad to Holland and Switzerland, not common in the dirt poor 1930s.

But the sea and ship theme never left and was nurtured through the years when my parents went regularly on summer holidays to the town of Kirn on the Clyde estuary.

Listening to Old George, the local boatman, I learned to name every one of the many Clyde paddle steamers that came regularly alongside the Kirn pier. Many of my days were spent helping George patch up his rowing boats which summer visitors endeavored, unwittingly I suppose, to reduce to matchwood. I, of course, did not consider myself a summer visitor, and proudly, for me, neither did George. He had known me since the age of 2 when my parents would occasionally take me for a short trip around the Holy Loch on his motor launch.

I owe a lot to George. He taught me seamanship as it should be taught—in a small boat. In later years when I brought a destroyer alongside another ship or dock, it was with far less difficulty than I timidly edged George's launch, against his rickety old jetty.

In my mid-teens, my weekends were spent at, and on Loch Lomond, sailing a 16-footer, courtesy of my nonconforming scoutmaster, Captain Arthur B. "Puddock" Wright, a World War I fighter pilot who had the distinction, or so it was considered, of being shot down by German ace, Baron Manfred von Richthofen. Wright escaped with leg wounds; Richtofen was shot down and killed in 1918.

Nearing my 18th birthday I realized three things, (1) I was not a scholar, (2) war was coming, and (3) I wanted freedom from the confinement of an office. Whether it was seeing another movie or reading the life of Lord Northcliffe of *London Times* fame I'm unsure, but I decided to try for journalism.

I was lucky. I was given an introduction, through friends, to the editor of Glasgow's powerful conservative newspaper, *The Glasgow Herald*, who told me that no job was presently available but if I could do 120 words a minute in shorthand and type 80 words a minute he'd give me one. Three months later, after intensive courses at a commercial college where I was only one of two men among 25 women and girls, I produced the necessary certificate. He kept his word.

My beginning was at the bottom. There were eight of us on the telephone staff, six by day and two by night. We were the telephone stenographers of the paper's outlying correspondents and reporters on assignment. All news not handled by the wire or news agencies came through us. It may not sound interesting, but to a youth of 18 it held a certain amount of glamour. When a big story was being phoned in we would be at the centre of attention. Agitated sub-editors, hoping to catch the first edition, would stand over us grabbing each page when completed. One "quiet" from us as we endeavored to pick up some distorted reporter's voice over our headphone set would silence the most garrulous sub-editor. From telephone clerk to typesetter, each at one point, adds his part to the completed article on the conveyor belt. The newspaper office demands this and the ink scratchers love it. To me it was the first example of teamwork, outside of games, and a lesson I was not to forget.

As potential journalists of the future, we were not held rigidly to one job. The lesser theatre criticisms fell our way as well as the covering of junior sports games and our own offerings of articles and gossip paragraphs. We did very well on these sidelines, and as each success assured a little extra money, there was plenty of competition. Ever seeking ways and means of getting into print,

I decided I would try and cover the World Scout Jamboree to be held in Holland in the summer of 1937. Having earlier belonged to a scout troop, I had no difficulty in joining the Scottish contingent travelling to Holland which consisted of more than 2,000 boys. The paper promised to consider any material I should send and so began my first legitimate assignment.

The Jamboree, which was held near the Hague, consisted of thousands of tents and thousands of boys of all nationalities. Here, for the last time, I was to see the boys who were to be the soldiers of tomorrow. Our own British tommys, airmen and sailors, the American G.I. and the gallant Poles and Norwegians. They were all blissfully unaware of their future. I often wonder of those 50,000 boys how many are alive today—how many may have suffered the horrors of the concentration camp, the jungles and the killing. The two contingents who might have prevented that future were not there—the Germans and the Japanese. They were not there because the growing war machine of their respective countries had already enslaved them. The division of the coming war was already clear in that World Scout Jamboree, but few realized it.

I did not think of war as I photographed the Palace of Peace at the Hague one day. Nor did I think of it as 10,000 Scouts, representing seven nations, sat round a campfire one evening and in turns broadcast to their respective countries. For 14 days, 50,000 boys were united under one leader, Lord Baden-Powell, and for 14 days 50,000 boys sang one song—"the Jamboree Song." A tune with a lilting melody which could be heard whistled, hummed or sung all over Holland during their stay. My writings to the paper were an 17-year-old's conception of a mass demonstration of youths' internationalism—and so it appeared. The Jamboree was a success and so in a small way was my coverage for the paper.

The threat of war was already creeping into the press when I returned. A year later the Munich crisis followed and passed. The peace-lovers reverted to their old slogans, but the press endeavored to stir the "ostriches." In the hubbub of the sub-editors and reporters' room, war was only a matter of time. As we followed Hitler's marching armies from Czechoslovakia to Poland, the tension in the news room could be felt. Here as nowhere else, one could feel the pulsing heart of nerve-racked Europe. As copy boys passed flimsy sheets of wire agency flashes to the waiting sub-editor handling "Europe", his expression was studied by other strained faces. The war of nerves had begun here too—and it was no phony war.

By February 1939 the vast majority considered war inevitable. Government pamphlets were already circulating for potential air raid wardens, ambulance drivers and volunteers for all services.

As a young reporter my duties took me to the night birds of Glasgow's one-and-a-quarter million population. Following up stories, I roved Glasgow's slums in the "wee" hours. Once my reward was a vicious hatchet murder. On another occasion, two drunks who had burned to death in a rooming house bed through a carelessly discarded cigarette. My casual acquaintances included prostitutes as well as policemen. I met all types at the widely scattered coffee stalls which drew together Glasgow's midnight prowlers. I was bona fide among habitues. I was just "the young reporter" and as such could talk to all, and good talk it often was. Police stations, hospitals, and fire stations were my beat. At every place veterans of World War I were holding forth on their own war experiences, giving advice, and those too young to serve in 1914 –18 were listening. They were listening and thinking—and I was one of them. I had many friends in the Central Police court, and if I was not following up some murder, fire, or theft story we would sit and chat.

It was here I decided to make my first overtures to the Navy, encouraged by a veteran of the battle of Jutland now Detective Sergeant McGuiness. In one government pamphlet I had noticed

Young reporter on the beat.

an appeal for amateur yachtsmen to join the Royal Naval Volunteer Reserve. After considerable correspondence and a warning to provide myself with several references, I was requested to attend the Royal Naval Volunteer Reserve headquarters, Clyde Division, for interview. The interview was successful, partly because I had previously taken the trouble to attend classes on Navigation at the Royal Technical College of Glasgow. This enabled me to answer quickly and accurately two rather simple navigational questions. I also, I gather, proved that I knew something of small boats which was substantiated by a yachting friend already enrolled as an officer.

My future was now clear and I attended my navigational classes twice weekly and once a week attended signaling classes at Reserve Headquarters.

The inevitable occurred on Sept. 3, 1939—Britain was at war with Germany. My own reaction to that momentous moment was only one of excitement. I had known it would come and now that it had, I was eager to be in it; eager to put my recently acquired knowledge and myself to the test. I was neither frightened, worried or depressed, greatly contrasting, I am sorry to say, to my parents' mood. They could not understand their son being thus eager for war, but what parent can understand that war is a young man's greatest challenge? It is difficult for those who have suffered from war to realize that the young have to suffer also to prove the tragedy of war. While there is spirit and adventure in each generation of youth, they will be willing to fight for their country and for the right to live a free life. A boy's heroes are the characters he reads of—soldiers, sailors, airmen, and explorers. He follows through their trials and bears their hardships as his own—I did it with Scott and Oates, with Evans of the "Broke", Nelson and Grenville, and thousands of others. As long as the deeds of these men live, there will be others ready and willing to fight and die as they did.

In the early hours of the following morning, the news of the first blow struck against Britain came filtering through—the 13,000 ton liner, *S.S. Athenia*, had been torpedoed 250 miles north west of Ireland. I was alone on duty in the reporter's room at the time. Rumours had been coming in all night but it was not till 5:00 AM that we received definite confirmation from the wire agencies. I hastily recast the middle page to catch the last city edition and thus handled the first big story since Britain declared war.

As the months passed with no word from the Navy, I began to despair. Certainly the war did not materialize into the terrific battering ram that was expected but that was little solace to me. The sixty or so other members of the R.N.V.S.R. (Royal Navy Volunteer Supplementary Reserve) were equally disappointed. By November 2, 1939, two months after war had been declared, only six had left to begin their training at *H.M.S. King Alfred*, the naval establishment at Brighton. We were given various reasons for the delay in call-up by Captain Maurice Clark R.N.V.R., head of the Clyde division—lack of training facilities was the basic one. It was not till December 15th 1939 that the long buff-coloured envelope, "On His Majesty's Service", arrived. I was to report to *H.M.S. King Alfred* at noon on January 3rd 1940. There were other instructions regarding clothes and procedure. I would be enrolled as a temporary midshipman R.N.V.R. if I passed the medical examination and the final board. I was fortunate that two of us from Glasgow would be going together. George Wishart, who was my own age, and had joined at the same time was to be my shipmate for the next 3 months. He was only 5ft. 4ins. in height, but tough and keen and it was with deep regret I heard he had been lost in a convoy to Russia in 1943 when his ship was torpedoed. He was one of the many who gave their lives from our original 60 amateur yachtsmen.

I had plenty of time to prepare before leaving for Hove, adjacent to better known Brighton. I explained to my editor, that my call-up had come through and he thoroughly understood, giving good wishes and promising my job when I returned. No one could expect more; I was talking, however, to a man who had done exactly the same as I in World War I. I heard many stories later on similar farewells that were not as smooth.

George and I, two rather timorous civilians, were standing completely naked, being probed by a naval doctor. We were still confused. The minute we had stepped into *H.M.S. King Alfred* we had been saluted—not being altogether unmannerly we surreptitiously tried to return this, the result being a cross between scratching our foreheads and lifting our hats. Our efforts were greeted by controlled mirth from a group of young officers with the single gold lace wavy band of a Sub-Lieutenant (S/Lt) R.N.V.R. glinting on their sleeves. We dismissed them as morons of probably one week standing. Forms approached us from every angle after that with question upon question. The doctor having finished, we were all lined up—about 100 of us—for the final interview with the Commanding Officer of the station, Captain Pelly R.N. It was the medical report we were afraid of. Visualize returning home rejected as C3, it was a frightening thought. My interview lasted about 10 seconds and as I withdrew in a dazed condition, I realized I had become "the lowest form of animal life" in the Royal Navy—a midshipman R.N.V.R.

Not all were as lucky as George and I. We heard that about 40 had been rejected for various reasons—if true, a very high percentage. *H.M.S. King Alfred*, though named after a ship, which was the custom of the Royal Navy, was a shore station. It had been a small R.N.V.R. headquarters in peacetime. The beginnings of a vast luxury lido being constructed alongside had been requisitioned to enlarge the original. There were no sleeping quarters in either place and officers were boarded out in nearby hotels. There must have been 200 officers scattered around the vicinity. In the mornings we reported to *King Alfred*, had our meals and instruction there, and returned to our hotels in the evening. Very few of the new arrivals had purchased uniforms, as had been advised in the case of rejection, but in a weeks time most of us were presentable naval officers. We were divided into 10 groups of 20 according to our age and qualifications. I was one of the "middies" squad of about 23. We were warned that we would have about a 5-month period in front of us and in that time had to digest a normal midshipman's peacetime course of three years. Many of the older S/Lts, particularly those with master's or yachtsman's tickets, only remained for a week. One officer spent three days and on the fifth day was in command of a minesweeping trawler.

The officers in those early days were the cream of the reserve and were already semi-qualified. Many of them, though civilians, had done the annual fortnight's training cruise with the fleet. They were civilians, but reserve officers of as much as 15 years standing. We "middies" were not going to be thrust upon some hapless commanding officer with such speed. The older men were really pinch-hitting, while it was hoped we were to form the backbone of the reserve officers of the future. In other words, in all respects, apart from the R.N.V.R. status we would be capable of performing any duty that a fully-fledged naval officer of our own rank could do. That was the way it turned out.

In 1940 the mere thought of an R.N.V.R. officer being in command of a fleet destroyer or submarine—specialized branches of the Royal Navy would have been laughed at. By 1945 it was not uncommon. Trawlers, minesweepers, and later corvettes were, of course, their normal commands but those were minor war vessels—fleet units were a different category. In World War I, few R.N.V.R officers advanced from the small vessel class, but this time it was a different story. It had to be, with latterly 90 percent of the whole fleet, comprising reservists.

Our studies were carried out in what would have been the

larger parking garage of the Lido. This was used partly as protection against possible air raids. It consisted only of bare cement walls. There was no ventilation or heating. The only entrance for air was down the ramps leading underground and these let in plenty of air—cold, icy English Channel air. There were a few classrooms on the upper level and one or two below. The majority of the instruction, however, was carried out in the large underground garage space. A few benches and a black board in one corner and we were at work. It sometimes became so cold that the petty officer conducting instruction would be forced to run us around to warm up. Cement dust, which floated around was another worry. At the worst point a flu epidemic, which was ravaging the country struck us. More than 50 percent were affected at one period. Classes became very thin. As a precaution we were all lined up during the morning parade and had our throats sprayed with antiseptic. My roommate in the hotel was off for 10 days. George and I both caught it but managed to struggle along. Our poor instructors could hardly hear themselves speak above the barrage of coughs and sneezes.

As a bunch of 18 and 19-year-olds we were quite a handful at times for our instructors. One petty officer who taught us gunnery, repeated his lectures parrot fashion. There was nothing wrong with this, but we soon found, one interruption, and he had to start from the beginning again. He often had his revenge. The heavy gun battery where we practiced loading drill was situated near an open square of ground used for field training. He would march two guns crews to the middle of this field and then yell, "Guns crews close up." A mad stampede to the battery was the result. Instead of the large double doors leading to the battery being open, there was only one very small one. For two hectic minutes that one door resembled a bargain basement or a football scrum. We liked our P.O., however, and when by mistake—I repeat by mistake—a 60 lb. shell was dropped on his foot, one of us each day would visit him in the hospital. He trained nine of us into the best loading team that had as yet graced *King Alfred*.

In the evenings, which were our own, we would invade Brighton's nightspots. We all travelled around together, drank our small quantity of beer, danced, and had a thoroughly good time. A midshipman's pay of 5 shillings a day does not permit much more. We were popular and as yet neither Brighton's young female population nor restaurateurs had been swamped by the thousands yet to come. Midshipmen are the, "darlings of old ladies, but old ladies go to be bed at nine o'clock so their dreams are never shattered."

It was unfortunate that this was the coldest winter southern England had known for years. There was snow on the ground during the whole of February and the blizzards were accompanied by a freezing north wind. Rifle drill on the snow-covered parade ground was a nightmare. Each time we "sloped arms," from the "ease," position the metal butts of the rifle would repose in our bare palm like an ice cube. We were too proud to wear gloves. The midshipmen had the reputation of being a tough bunch and we were determined not to break it.

At the end of March our first trip to sea as naval officers was arranged. An ex-private yacht had been taken over by the navy and lay at Newhaven—peacetime cross channel port. As we left by bus for Newhaven, a strong breeze was blowing up. Someone suddenly thought of the idea of putting everyone's name into a hat. It cost 1 shilling to draw a name and the one who held the name of the first person to be seasick would win the lot, happy little playmates that we were. After the ragging had died down a little, most were becoming visibly introspective. I realized I had missed my breakfast and had been up till 1:00 AM the night before—anything but a good omen.

We were all rather subdued as we boarded the yacht and realized it was blowing a near gale outside. Whether to toughen us up, or whether for U-boat safety, we lay just clear of the sand bar and rolled and pitched indescribably. We each took a "trick", at the wheel, gave orders to the helmsman, prepared the seaboat, made flag hoists, and read the Kelvin depth sounding gear. No one had as yet been sick but some were turning a very green colour and the respective ticket holders were encouraging their men with stories of greasy bacon and swinging lanterns. Quite suddenly I began to feel ill and then began a terrific inward fight to control it. I went through agonies, but fortunately for my self-respect I came out second. The whole business quite evidently had only required a start. After that there were only about 3 people not affected and one of them was George who also held the winning ticket. First out was a midshipman named Elgar, now holder of the Distinguished Service Cross. For two hours we carried on with our duties and it was simply hell. I may say this many times to come but I will begin now—an officer or rating who is in the slightest way addicted to sea-sickness and carries on with his duties has the guts of a lion.

I have seen men in an Atlantic gale so physically and mentally exhausted by sickness that they would have rolled off the deck into the sea without putting out a hand to save themselves. Let all people realize that, 99 times out of 100, sailors' greatest fight is still against the sea whether by sickness or hardship—at least in small ships. I knew of one destroyer captain who had a bucket on the bridge beside him every time his ship left harbour. If the weather were rough he would be unable to eat, yet he carried out his duties in the ordinary way. That requires more courage and grit than facing the enemy. He could have applied for transfer to bigger ships on the grounds of sickness but he didn't. He was a trained destroyer captain, this was his job, and he would do it. It was a happy but thoughtful group of midshipmen who left their first experience of the sea behind them, some no doubt thinking the Army might have been better after all.

Our examinations were over by the beginning of April and all we now awaited was our appointment to a ship. Twice a week appointments were put on the notice boards and we longingly looked for our names. It was not till April 14th that I learned I was bound for a drifter, *H.M.D. Seabreeze,* at Scapa Flow. Four of our class were appointed to the mighty battle cruiser, *H.M.S. Hood,* and two years later all four were lost when the *Hood* was sunk in an engagement with the German battleship *Bismark.* At the time we were envious of those four—later we were sorry. The vast percentage of the midshipmen were sent to drifters or trawlers, a few to motor torpedo boats, but as yet this force was still in its infancy.

Jan. 1940, King Alfred Training Centre, Hove, England, (Ian, bottom right).

Morning Run, King Alfred Training Centre, 1940.

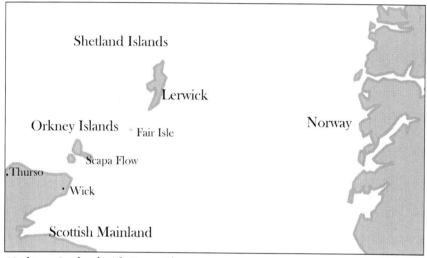

Norhtern Scotland with Scapa Flow.

CHAPTER 2

SCAPA FLOW

Scapa Flow is Britain's northernmost naval base. It is practically a small inland sea surrounded by the islands of the Orkney group. To the north lie the Shetland Islands and further north still the Faros and Iceland. It was to Orkney and Scapa Flow I was bound. My commanding officer and I left *King Alfred* together, he as a Lieutenant and I as a Sub/Lieutenant.

The trip from Brighton to Scrabster, northernmost port of Scotland, was long and tedious. It is one of the few train journeys in Britain which occupy two nights and practically two days travelling. The famous train "The Jellicoe", named in the First World War, completed the last part of the journey from Perth. The train was run by the Navy and used mainly by the Services. Every officer and rating, apart from the privileged few who flew, traveled by "The Jellicoe" to reach the Orkneys. The whole area north of Inverness was restricted and travel for civilians limited. From Scrabster we bucked through the fast running Pentland Firth in the little steamer *St. Ninian* which did the round trip once a day from Scapa Flow to the mainland. We tied up alongside the depot ship *Proserpine* in the middle of an air raid. The war had begun for us but there was little to see. Air raids at Scapa were a common occurrence in those early days especially if some of the heavier fleet units were lying at anchor. As often as not they were precautionary enemy planes on reconnaissance flights. From *Proserpine* we were transferred to *H.M.S. Iron Duke*—a veteran battleship of the last war now being used as a base and dispersal ship. We eagerly searched for the name of *Seabreeze* on the drifters lying alongside the *Iron Duke* but with no result. Later we learned our trip had been in vain. *Seabreeze* was refitting at the small Scottish east coast fishing town of Fraserburgh.

We remained on *Iron Duke* for a week and during that period there were six air raids. The first time German planes flew over we stood on deck and gazed happily upwards watching the fun. We had to be practically driven below by an irate petty officer muttering "of all the bloody fools, they'll get killed soon enough without hanging out a sign." We had seen our first bomb drop and had felt the ship shiver from the blast of a near miss—we were very happy. I must say I was remarkably unimpressed. It was only when we were led down into the bowels of the *Iron Duke* during a later raid that I had any feeling of nervousness. The idea of the mass of pipes and machinery surrounding me—the ominous closing of hatch after hatch as we descended gave the dread feeling of being trapped. There and then I decided to avoid large ships and fortunately never had to repeat the experience. I have always been able to stand on the deck, the bridge or gun mounting when bombs were to fall in the future.

Before I visited Scapa Flow the name alone intrigued me. I knew this was where the German High Seas Fleet scuttled themselves in 1918. I also knew it was synonymous with British Sea Power. The name itself had a feeling of "the silent service" and its geographical position added to this feeling of mystery. Scapa Flow was, as I had imagined, bleak and windswept. The islands rose gently towards the center like small mounds—never, however, attaining any height. The color was grayish, due to the rocky nature of the ground and the sparse, scrubby grass that was all that could survive there. There were no trees or bushes. The small, cultivated parts adjoining the scattered farms appeared ashamed to be there.

It was the Flow itself which was impressive. Launches, pinnaces (tenders) and drifters were continuously plying to and from the larger fleet units. Battleships, cruisers, destroyers and aircraft carriers lay somberly in their dark battleship grey. At the head of Longhope Sound lay supply ships and oilers of all descriptions. At the main pier, drifters pushed and nosed each other around as they arrived or left with stores and men. Behind the pier the construction of large sheds, storerooms and recreation rooms was under way. An odd Army uniform could be seen mixing with navy blue soldiers coming in to make a few purchases before returning to their anti-aircraft sites. One had to walk around the islands to discover the strength of anti-aircraft defenses. The only way to discover a gun emplacement was to fall into it—I literally did that on two occasions. All visitors are welcome at those gun sites, however, even if they do arrive face down. Any news from "outside"— peculiarly enough that means Britain, of which Orkney is a part—is eagerly sought. To live the life of an Army gunner, anchored to the one spot for months on end, one has to be either monastic or ingenious.

My commanding officer and I were now informed that *Seabreeze* had been located in the east coast village of Fraserburgh and we proceeded there by way of Glasgow. Once we arrived we put up in one of the two hotels and decided to move round to the "local" and see what news of *Seabreeze* we could pick up. Fraserburgh is primarily a small fishing port. The people there, catch fish, eat fish and talk fish. The men, by themselves, talk boats—the boats that catch the fish Seine-netters, drifters and deep sea trawlers. We were both Scotsmen, and though not fishermen, this fact was sufficient to break the ice.

To our surprise we were already known. In a short time we knew our drifter had been built for the Navy as such. It was all steel whereas the ordinary fishing drifters were built of wood. We learned, however, they liked our engines and on the whole were complimentary. The proceedings had been rather grotesque. Here we were, two naval officers, having our ship, as yet unseen, described to us by fishing and trawler crews; not only our ship but our crew went under review. We discovered they had all gone to a dance at the nearby town of Peterhead. Our coxswain was a Fraserburgh man and therefore merited special attention which he got. It was not all complimentary.

There were still about five of us remaining in the pub when closing time arrived. This seemed to cause no inconvenience. We went out of the front door and returned by the back to a private room, and the beer and conversation continued unabated. One of the local constables joined us later—perhaps to put everything on a lawful footing.

Early next morning we were down at the fish quays, and alongside one lay His Majesty's drifter *Seabreeze*. She was much the same as the twenty or so other drifters in the harbor, apart from her paint of battleship grey, her small 3-pdr-gun standing defiantly on a raised platform at the bow, and the rather dirty and tattered white ensign which flew from her mizzen mast. A rather grimy and disheveled object appeared from the galley entrance aft and my C.O.—now at a low ebb—bawled sufficiently hard to "bring him up all standing." He was the cook, and in true naval fashion had been detailed as "the watch" by the coxswain for the night. He answered the C.O.'s questions but volunteered nothing. I am sure he was unconvinced of our authenticity. He confirmed the crew had left for Peterhead the previous evening and should be back soon. We decided we would await their return and after that Lt. Kemp, my C.O., decided to bewail the horrible truth of chaos to the nearest naval authority at Peterhead.

Our crew arrived shortly; a very dejected bunch of men led by what we presumed was our coxswain, dressed in a fisherman's roll neck jersey and petty officers cap. After much questioning we learned the crew had been "standing by" for a week. They had been entirely on their own, there being no supervising officer in Fraserburgh. They were all new to the ship and had been awaiting our arrival and that of the engineer petty officer. Kemp left me with several of the crew to clean the ship, while he took our coxswain, Buller, to one side and did quite a bit of hard and fast-talking.

"Our drifter crew arrived!"

Our Drifter crew arrived!

Seabreeze was practically devoid of stores. A local ship chandler was under naval contract, and I shortly presented him with an imposing list of essentials, varying from life belts to three-inch manila ropes. This order was carried out with amazing rapidity and within a week *Seabreeze* was as ship-shape as any drifter can possibly be. Our instructions were to proceed to Peterhead where we would be issued with ammunition, charts, and all stores would be checked.

The advent of our leaving proved quite an occasion and many of the fishermen and the coxswain's wife and children were there to wave goodbye. My C.O. had placed Buller in the wheelhouse, myself on the bow and chose the little bridge above the wheelhouse for his own place of vantage. It may seem odd to say he chose the bridge because by naval standards the bridge is his rightful place, but it must be remembered a drifter is not the textbook version of a naval vessel and frequently the bridge is never used. We left without undue embarrassment apart from a few bumps

Playing 'Old Sea Dog' in wheelhouse of Seabreeze.

HMD Seabreeze.

against the quay-sides leading out of the inner dock. A final fare-well screech on the siren, which the coxswain insisted on for good luck, and we were off.

The passage to Peterhead was uneventful and the two days spent there were occupied with a routine check of stores, and some gunnery instruction. Our ship's company comprised eleven ratings and two officers. Our two engineers, both Lowestoft men, knew their job well. They had both been engineers in fishing drifters for years. They were already known as "chief" and "seconds" according to their seniority. There was one gunnery rating and one signalman—both Londoners. Our three seamen were from St. Johns, Newfoundland, all fishermen who had volunteered at the outbreak of hostilities. One known as "Butch" is one of the few men I have seen lift a depth charge weighing some 450 lbs clear of the deck single-handed. Two stokers and our coxswain completed the ships complement. The armament consisted of one 3-pdr-gun, one Lewis machine gun, one Vickers belt-fed of

1912 vintage and four depth charges. The Vickers intrigued me and for the length of my stay on *Seabreeze* I was the only one who could nurse a tune from it.

We left for Scapa on the third day in very bad weather. The coxswain and I were at loggerheads over navigation on this our first trip. He would have nothing to do with my charts on which I had proudly laid the various courses off. He reckoned he could smell his way to Scapa more accurately than I could chart it. Without either giving way, we decided if his sense of smell disagreed with my courses we would reconsider any future move. We arrived at Scapa without any reconsidering and berthed alongside *Iron Duke*. For a week we pottered around the Flow while the gunnery and signal ratings absorbed a little more instruction.

At the end of the week we were onward routed farther northward to Lerwick in the Shetland Islands. The trip was not without incident. First we struck the Pentland Skerries at the wrong turn of the tide. The six to eight knot current which runs through the Skerries left us lying entirely stationary for four hours. This upset our time schedule and the one light on the small island of Fair Isle, half way between Orkney and Shetland was not flashing as expected. Missing the light involved us in a three-day trip without the assistance of any fix on land. This would have mattered little if we had had either a log or a sextant, but we had neither. I had requested both but with no result. I was therefore forced to navigate by dead reckoning, which in a ship making only six knots and encountering three to four knot currents was liable to land us in Norway or Mid-Atlantic. I do not feel proud of my calculations because guesswork had to play a large part, but on the morning of the third day the large bluff of Sumburgh Head, southernmost tip of Shetland, came into sight on the correct bearing—the port bow. The coxswain was convinced this landfall was due to his sense of smell but was gracious enough to give me some credit. The same evening we were securely moored alongside the fish wharf at Lerwick.

Lerwick was to be our base in the future. It was a quaint little town—a mixture of narrow paved streets, attractive old fashioned little houses, and modern roads and bungalows. Many of the people were of Scandinavian origin though the islands are Scottish. The islands are represented in Parliament by one member. The main industry is fishing. During the herring season, hundreds of drifters would lie at the fish piers and the fish girls from England and Scotland would also be there gutting, cleaning and salting. The war had brought this busy industry to an end. It was only an occasional drifter or trawler with a Government permit to fish outside the restricted areas which arrived with a load of fish.

The Royal Navy was represented by four ships in all at Lerwick. Two drifters—*Seabreeze* and *Harmattan*—and two smaller seine-net fishing vessels. It was not an impressive fleet and certainly not an offensive one. Our duties, however, were not offensive— they were defensive. At the northwestern tip of Shetland lay Sullom Voe, a long inlet with a large anchorage at the upper end. This anchorage was protected by an anti-U boat net. Inside, destroyers and cruisers could refuel from an oiler which was always in attendance. Our job was to patrol outside the net, identify approaching ships, and lead in those paying their first visit. We were supported on land by heavy gun batteries which covered the approaches. There was also an R.A.F. Coastal Command Sunderland base in the Voe. Landings in Norway were underway at that period and many of the destroyers taking part called in at Sullom to refuel. The anti-aircraft cruiser *Coventry* provided A/A (anti-aircraft) defense for the Voe. Occasionally a few German planes would make a bombing attack on the ships lying at anchor, but serious damage was never inflicted. The attacking planes never bothered us with larger targets on hand.

Normally one drifter and one seine-netter would patrol for three days, and at the end of that period would be relieved by the other two ships. Weather was so fierce at times, that we had to remain for a week to ten days on patrol before making the exposed passage back to Lerwick. On these occasions our stores were replenished from the Army base or brought over land.

During the British evacuation from Norway, we patrolled outside Lerwick to the east. It was mainly a precautionary measure in case of a sea attack. On the approach of hostile forces we were to fire a predetermined set of colored "Very Lights" (illuminating shells) and inform base by wireless. Our main excitement was contacting the many small Norwegian fishing vessels crowded with women and children who had made the rough passage to escape German domination. Many of them endured untold hardships to make the crossing. Some came by sail alone. Others began their trip in motorboats, but when fuel ran out used blankets as sails to complete the voyage. Many of the Norwegians who later formed the "underground" in Norway were among those first evacuees.

Some weeks later, while on patrol at Sullom, we were surprised to hear the sound of low flying aircraft—not the familiar roar of R.A.F. Sunderlands. As a precaution we closed up our small armament and awaited events. The planes were flying straight down the Voe but due to their low height it was impossible to distinguish their markings. They looked to me remarkably like German Heinkel 117 seaplanes. There was something about the way they approached which made me refrain from giving the order to open fire. They were now only a matter of feet above the sea and plainly waggling their wings—it was then I caught sight of the German crosses. It was too late to do anything as they had already landed. We approached with an R.A.F. launch which had put out from shore. The men were standing on the plane's floats yelling and waving. Cautiously we drew alongside and one man in broken English told us they were Norwegians and had stolen the two seaplanes from the Germans. The R.A.F. took charge of both men and planes and we never did get the full story, but they were both courageous and lucky men. Lucky to make their escape and lucky not to be blown to pieces by the shore batteries in the Voe. It so happened that we had lain between the gunners line of fire and the landing planes.

A possible German invasion of Shetland was now anticipated after the occupation of Norway, and coastal defense positions were increased and a curfew came into effect throughout the island. If in harbour, our orders were, in the event of invasion, to render the 3-pdr -gun useless and with the two machine guns and ammunition join the Army forces (Gordon Highlanders) garrisoned on the island, which at that time was under the Administration for Defense of Admiral of the Fleet the Earl of Cork and Orrery. The code word for invasion was "blood red" and we exercised mock attacks twice. No doubt the spectacle of *Seabreeze*'s complement loaded down with machine guns, ammunition, and tin hats, running through the streets of Lerwick caused some amusement, as did the admiral also parading clad in full regalia. But the islanders were seriously worried.

The admiral was in fact quite a character. One day we were informed that he would hoist his admiral's pennant on *Seabreeze*. I don't know if historically an admiral's pennant had ever before been flown on a beat up old drifter but it did on *Seabreeze*. We didn't have a clue as to the procedure but the admiral's flag lieutenant, not the admiral himself, showed up one morning with the flag which we saluted and hoisted to the amusement of our two stokers clad in dirty overalls. We asked the flag lieutenant the point of all this.

"Well," he said, "this allows the admiral to get extra sea-going money."

I suppose even noble admirals have to watch their finances.

On another occasion we got instructions that the admiral wanted us to carry out a depth charge attack. I asked Lt. Kemp if he thought the admiral meant a real live exercise, because I warned him, having had training in depth charges as a 90-day wonder (midshipman training), that as our drifter could barely do 6 knots it was not an ideal platform for hurling depth charges around.

The answer was "Do it!"

Came the big day, I set the charge to the greatest depth possible. It went off beautifully. Some 450 pounds of TNT exploded; a huge wave arose, picked up our stern and sent us hurtling forward like a surfer heading for the beach.

The next thing I saw was our chief engineer standing on deck, waving his fists and yelling blue murder. The sudden surge had thrown open the fire door in his engine room and hurled hot coals onto the grating and around his feet. That was our last depth charge exercise, but not the end of comic opera interludes.

This whole craziness was hard to believe. First off, our crew had no naval training. Lt. Kemp had about one week's instruction because of a yachting and reserve background, which hardly told him anything about guns, depth charges or naval discipline. I, as a mere midshipman and the youngest person on the ship, was the one person, as a 90-day wonder, who had had any instruction in gunnery, depth charges, navigation and naval discipline. As a mere 19-year-old midshipman I really had little authority, except back up from Lt. Kemp, to argue with the 50-year-old coxswain about navigation. And the Navy hadn't helped. First of all they lost our ship, followed by sending us on our way at the wrong turn of the tide and gave no warning that the light on Fair Isle was out.

And at one point in this epic, we were informed in a radio message that we were to leave Sullom Voe and keep a lookout for the German battleship *Tirpitz*. It so happened that it was blowing a full gale that day right down the Voe and we couldn't make any headway; in fact we barely managed to turn around and seek some shelter.

It was truly unbelievable but that was what happened on some ships in some placed in the 1940s and beyond. The foul-ups never halted, the comic interludes continued.

It was shortly after this my Commanding Officer left leaving me in command of *Seabreeze*. Patrols continued uneventfully and the greatest drawback proved to be monotony. Even on that small ship I couldn't become too familiar with the ratings. In my own small quarters I was often extremely lonely and though I shared watches with the coxswain 24-hours a day, I was bored. I felt my war effort, though perhaps essential, was not particularly glamorous, and I asked the base captain if I could not be transferred to destroyers—my greatest wish.

I hated, in my little drifter, to watch those sleek, graceful craft gliding past the boom to refuel. They always gave a cheery wave of thanks as I led them through the double row of nets but in my envy I interpreted condescension in that wave.

In September of 1940 Lt. Kemp returned after medical treatment and I was sent on leave pending re-appointment thanks to my base captain. For a month no news arrived, then once again the "buff envelope", and I was bound for *H.M.S. Black Bear* to join at Ardrossan on the Firth of Clyde.

Crew of HMD Seabreeze.

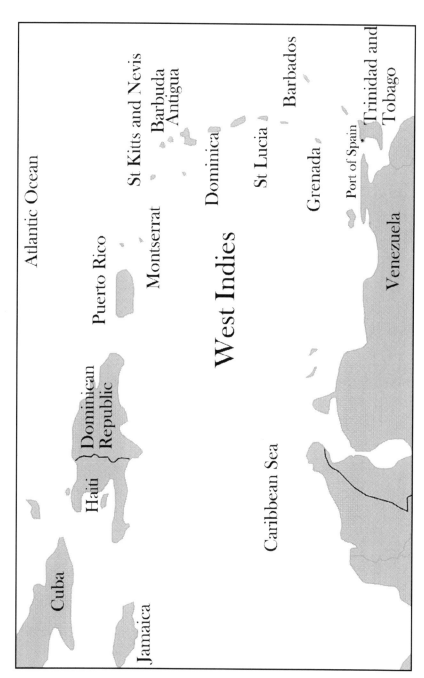

Map of the West Indies, showing Port of Spain, homeport of Black Bear.

CHAPTER THREE

TO THE WEST INDIES

Arriving at Ardrossan, I reported to the duty officer my name and the ship I was to join. He looked at me queerly.

"Did you say the *Black Bear*?"

When I replied in the affirmative he roared with laughter. I could see nothing particularly funny about this and he realized, I think, one more guffaw and something quite un-naval like might happen.

"My dear chap," he began, "the *Black Bear* is by now only some 100 miles east of Bermuda and will be there in the morning—how does that strike you?"

I felt any privilege of striking was more on my side but refrained from comment.

"Let's see your papers anyway."

I produced them and he agreed they were correct and suggested some blundering fool at the Admiralty had forgotten to move *Black Bear*'s pin away from Ardrossan.

"How does that affect me?" I asked.

"Do you want to go to Bermuda?" he shot back.

I hesitated, while sunny beaches and waving palm trees flitted through my brain and decided—yes.

"All right, go back on leave and I'll see what we can do."

On leave at home I wondered if I had done the right thing. The *Black Bear* was not a destroyer; it was an ex-luxury yacht belonging to Singer of sewing machine fame. Bermuda was rather a backwater as far as the war was concerned. It looked as though I had changed dirty water without finding any clean but the thing was done—you can't change your mind in the Navy.

I waited about a month before starting on the first lap of the journey to join *Black Bear*. At Greenock I embarked on the 17,000 ton Canadian Pacific Liner, *Duchess of York*. The ship was crowded with all three services. There were veteran pilots of Battle of Britain fame going to Canada as instructors, army officers—British and European—on their way to form the nucleus of new training units. The naval personnel were joining ships in Canada or the West Indies. In addition to service personnel, there were 2,000 German prisoners on board bound for Canadian POW camps.

For three days we watched the assembly of ship upon ship around us, and on the fourth day, we steamed down the Firth of Clyde as a massive convoy. On the fifth day, we were all back in harbour. U-boats, we understood, had been waiting for us off Ireland and it had been considered advisable for destroyers to break up this formation before we passed through the danger area.

Two days later we were off again, and the following morning, looking round the convoy, we realized what was at stake. There were 21 liners, not one of them under 17,000 tons. Our escort was large and in the middle of the convoy steamed the 30,000-ton veteran battleship *H.M.S. Ramilles*. The largest convoy to sail from Britain to that date was on the high seas.

The liners were packed with troops bound for the middle-east and Wavell's Army of the Nile. It was one of the most impressive sights I have ever witnessed. I have seen larger convoys at North Africa but never one composed entirely of ships of such size, each name familiar the world over. In that convoy sailed the

HMS Black Bear, Singer's (of sewing machine fame) ex-luxury yacht, Xarifa.

pride of Britain's Merchant Marine—and of the world—while below the sea sailed Germany's naval pride—the U-boat—waiting to destroy it.

We sailed north till it seemed we must have crossed the Arctic Circle, and then turned south. From the slow pitching deck of the *Duchess* it seemed all serene in the convoy with the escort destroyers faintly visible at two to three miles distance.

The occasional thud of a distant depth charge, however, reminded us that the U-boats were lurking and only those destroyers kept them away. The battleship was there to protect us from any German raider or pocket battleship which might be lurking. The gallant fight of the *Jervis Bay* in defense of her convoy against two German battleships was at the time only weeks old. The Admiralty were taking all precautions against a similar incident.

West of the Azores, we and the battleship *Ramilles* left for Halifax, Canada, while the remainder of the convoy continued their voyage round the Cape to Egypt. With no escort vessels, we were to dash for port at high speed, but gale weather prevented this. For two days we were reduced to 4 knots while the *Ramilles* repaired gale damage and prevented more.

There were many comments passed on the unseaworthiness of our older dreadnoughts—and with some justification too. *Ramilles* was continually awash and had she made more speed, the increased force and weight of water already completely obscuring her at times, would have done untold damage. Had any U-boat spotted us we were done, but the bad weather was equally in our favour. In those mountainous seas, a U-boat seeks depth for comfort. Many on board claimed that the German prisoners we carried would be our protection, but I doubted it. U-boat warfare in the Atlantic was directed by Admiral Karl Doenitz, whose policy was "ruthless extermination".

We arrived at Halifax safely. Six of us were proceeding to the West Indies and we spent six days too many in cold, unfriendly Halifax, before leaving for Boston and the British West Indies in the *S.S. Lady Hawkins*. We were not permitted ashore at Boston, the United States being neutral, but lying alongside at the wharf, we were subjected to the inquiring glances of passing dockers and officials. To them we were people from another world—a world at war, and America at that time was purely curious. Boston meant little to me then, but I could not see five years ahead. In 1945 I married my charming wife, and Boston is now my second home.

The voyage to Trinidad, I still feel, was sinful in a world at war. It was so beautiful, so comfortable and pleasant. We wandered down through the islands, stopping a day here and a day there. First Bermuda, where I received instructions to continue to Trinidad, then St. Kitts, Nevis, Antigua, Montserrat, Dominica, St Lucia, Barbados and Grenada. We had time to go ashore at each port of call, and I had my first initiation into the tropics. I was a wary initiate, I'm afraid, and possibly denied myself considerable pleasure by being so. I was germ conscious: afraid to drink out of glasses at the little restaurants, afraid of the smells, afraid of infection. I behaved as most people on their first visit to the tropics. My only defense was on medical grounds. I had not yet received injections against typhoid, malaria or yellow fever. I felt rather like a battleship without guns.

At Montserrat I experienced my first earthquake. A party of us drove across the small island and midway our coloured driver stopped.

"Get out," he said. "Feel earthquake."

Sure enough, we did. Just a tremor but perceptible. It is said Montserrat has a tremor once a day and two on Sundays. At St. Nevis we saw the little church where Nelson married Mrs. Nisbet. At St. Lucia we heard calypso singers—the attractive song melody peculiar to the B.W.I. A passenger boarding at Barbados gave me my first taste of pure white rum brewed by the monks living on the island of Dominica. We passed close to the Vichy fortress island of Martinique. It was a continuous succession of new experiences and new sights. The islands themselves were memorable, many of volcanic origin, dome-shaped and covered with thick green vegetation. The water was blue—a true blue—and clear, and the sandy beaches a beautiful golden color.

The West Indies are one of the few places where beauty and glamour surpass the expectations. There is a careless, joyous spirit in the white and coloured people who live there which cannot be painted, written or filmed. It is an atmosphere which lives in the islands and one has to live there to capture it. The way people talk, the way they walk, their easy laughter, their love of music, dancing, and carnival, is all in the atmosphere. Work is secondary to pleasure and money is a hateful necessity. There is little money in the islands. The days of the wealthy planters are over and large fruit and cocoa estates are falling into neglect through lack of markets. Oil is the only wealth in the islands today but not a wealth that can be shared by all. The businessmen of the islands look for better times and for markets for the abundant supplies of cocoa and fruit which grow so easily there, but if those times are slow in coming they are not unduly upset.

I was to learn all this and much more during my stay in Trinidad, but I have to retrace my steps first and land. Port of Spain, seaport and capital of Trinidad provides a large natural anchorage for shipping in the Gulf of Paria. The anchorage is protected from the Caribbean by a string of islands stretching across the entrance. The channels between the islands are known as the Bocas. The dock area is small and cannot handle the larger types of ships. Those unable to go alongside are unloaded by lighter barges.

The *Lady Hawkins*, being a mail and supply ship, had docking preference. *H.M.S. Benbow,* the naval station, was on the waterfront and I reported my arrival there.

Once again disappointment. No one quite knew why I had come but, as I had, they thought something might as well be done about it. *Black Bear* evidently required no more officers, but I was instructed to report my arrival in any case. The ship was lying a few hundred yards along the quay and looking very much like the luxury yacht she had been before entering naval service. The captain did not seem at all pleased to see me, but I was allowed to remain until he discussed my future with the base commanding officer.

The captain's unfriendliness was not that of his officers, who plied me with questions of home and sympathized with my awkward predicament. In the morning I left my luxury cabin with private bath and reported to the base captain. He was understanding but plainly told me I was not for *Black Bear* at present. As an alternative he suggested—in the way a senior officer does—that I lend a hand as an instructing officer at Staubles training camp.

"We train the local volunteers out there," he said. "They are all coloured boys and you would prove most useful. It won't be difficult. You should have the up-to-date training methods at your fingertips being fresh from home."

That same afternoon I was on my way to Staubles in a naval van complete with baggage. The camp was about 15 miles north of Port of Spain directly opposite the islands leading to the Bay. It comprised two large wooden bungalows of two stories, one the wardroom and officers sleeping quarters, the other ratings. The camp was jammed between the single narrow cul-de-sac road, which ran a few miles further north, and the sea. On the land side of the road, dense bush covered the ground which rose steeply to the thickly wooded hills beyond. The wardroom, as in most tropical climes, was open on all four sides. There were eight officers at the base, the senior being a Lt. Commander R.N.V. R. Five of the officers and a handful of Royal Navy ratings supervised the anti-submarine detection loops which ran across the entrance to the Bay. The remaining three officers, all local T.R.N.V.R., were instructors. I arrived at the height of a crab hunt. The base was infested with large ugly land crabs which, though harmless, were becoming troublesome. Ratings and officers were darting about armed with sticks and wads of burning cotton waste. The crabs were being smoked out of their holes and then dispatched.

The hunt finished, the officers congregated in the wardroom, and I went through the now familiar procedure of a new arrival. As far as I could understand, my duties were simply as a watch-keeping officer. I would be on watch one day and off the following. My duty would entail supervising the ratings in the camp, checking routine "van" trips to Port of Spain and motor-boat schedules to the nearby islands. Not even any instructing. It was all rather depressing and disappointing.

After supper the officers gave me the low down on life at Staubles. It appeared to comprise a continuous fight against disease and animal life. The animal life I was discovering rapidly. The various diseases gave me the unusual urge for the feel of the doctors' hypodermic. I heard that malaria was a matter of course. There were lepers in the Indian villages and cases of elephantiasis. One of the nearby islands was a leper colony. Everyone suffered from foot rot and prickly heat. In the animal world there were scorpions, whose bite can be fatal if unattended; "vampire" bats which gently alight on an uncovered victim and suck the blood. As well, there were snakes and baboons, mosquitoes and chiggers, an insect which burrows under the skin and then lays its eggs.

The officers derived considerable amusement relating their stories—all for my benefit. I pretended to treat it all as a joke, but I was far from being amused. With a few parting remarks on sharks, electric eels, and stinging egg fish, I retired timorously to my room. The room contained a bed with, to my relief, a mosquito net, a few wooden shelves, a rather chipped basin and a cracked mirror. It would be impossible to re-enact that first night.

The boards between the rooms on my level and the wardroom beneath were cracked and gaping—an insect's paradise. I lifted one of my cases from the floor and a cockroach as big as a small mouse scurried away. There was a continuous hum of insect life from the bush outside, and one or two mosquitoes were already "stunting" round my ears. The holes in the window mesh I stuffed with odd pieces of cloth. For half an hour I diligently drew together the mosquito net over my bed with needle and thread. I looked under the pillow on the bed to discover another mouse-size cockroach which I unfortunately stood on and I swear I heard bones crack. Eventually I climbed into bed, carefully tucking the netting all round me, and tried to sleep. It was hopeless.

The tin roof above my head resounded to a continuous pattering—bats, I remembered from the after-supper conversation.

A disquieting steady hum interspersed with an odd screech floated in from the bush beyond. I dozed away and eventually was shaken awake by a black steward the next morning at 6:30. I dressed slowly, shaking every article of clothing and examining my shoes for a possible scorpion, but fortunately there were no alarms.

Arising early, as I was duty officer for the day, I found myself first for breakfast. Walking across to the breakfast table, I noticed to my horror an animal sitting in one of the chairs. To me it resembled a small dragon and further than that I will not go. I heard the steward pottering around in the kitchen at the rear and, being no St George, hastily called him. I pointed at "the thing" and he whispered me outside. He disappeared for a few seconds, returning with another rating holding a blanket. The two of them plus blanket, crept up behind "the thing" and with a sudden lunge ensnared it. Carrying away the struggling animal, which must have weighed at least 15 lbs., they disappeared into the kitchen. There it was dispatched and the steward served my breakfast and offered an explanation. The animal was an iguana, a member of the lizard family—nasty-looking, but perfectly harmless. Trinidadians consider it a luxury food as it makes excellent soup, and the flesh, I was told, tastes exactly like chicken.

That was a bad start to the morning, but only a foretaste. I had been told two old Royal Navy pensioners, now living in Trinidad, assisted as instructors at the camp. Towards noon I met them probing around bushes armed with forked sticks and accompanied by a bull terrier.

"Still crab hunting?" I asked.

"No," one replied, "snakes this time."

Sure enough the dog started barking and from below a nearby bush a snake glided out. As I also glided out, I saw the snake pinioned with the forked stick by one and its head being battered by another. Heavenly days—but not for me.

I spent a week at Staubles and was thoroughly miserable the

whole time. Months later I returned and spent a most enjoyable three days leave. My initiation to the tropics and its fauna was too rapid for my wellbeing at the time.

The rapid change of policy which sent me hurriedly back from Staubles to join *Black Bear* as a watch-keeping officer, within a week, is one of those unfathomable naval idiosyncrasies which just happen. A naval officer is forever in the "dark" on two subjects, firstly his movements, secondly his pay. It is a sheer waste of time to puzzle out either.

Black Bear followed a steady weekly routine—patrolling six days out of seven between Tobago and Trinidad and acting as rescue and sighting ship for Fleet Air Arm pilots. The pilots trained at the naval air station, *H.M.S. Goshawk*, 12 miles south of Port of Spain. Our work was uninteresting but pleasant enough. We lay up evenings at Mt. Irvine Bay, Tobago. Flying was generally over by 4 in the afternoon, and we had time for a pleasant swim after reaching our anchorage. Sometimes we might walk ashore in the evenings or merely sit and drink and listen to a gramophone on the awning-covered sun deck of *Black Bear*. Tourists would have paid hundreds of pounds to do what we were doing for nothing. It still did not compensate for the boredom.

One interesting experience was a docking visit to the Dutch island of Curacao. Docking was necessary and Willemstad at Curacao was the one place at hand which could cope with a ship of our size.

The town of Willemstad is divided by a narrow neck of water which leads to the inner harbour. Joining the two parts of the town is a bridge supported by a series of 15 pontoon boats. When a ship is about to enter, the pontoons and bridge swing open like a file of precision soldiers doing a left turn. The power is derived from the end pontoon which is engined. To watch the bridge swing open is rather a mystery at first. The local people are very proud of their bridge, which I believe is the only one of its kind in the world.

Willemstad is a considerable port and can take in ships up to 20,000 tons. The island itself has the largest oil refineries in the West Indies. The oil is shipped across in specially constructed shallow draught vessels from Venezuela and refined in Curacao. The island is permeated with the smell of oil. Ship building and repairs are quite extensive at the yards. For the first time since visiting the B.W.I., I heard the familiar ring of rivet and hammer—a homely noise to a Clydesider.

The Dutch living in the islands are very Dutch, reserved and rather suspicious. There were, we knew, anti-British elements in the city but they were not obvious. In fact, little was obvious, as we were left severely alone.

The city was clean and quite attractive, though as with most towns with a coloured population, it had its slum district. Entertainment among the Dutch was mostly carried out in the home. There were, however, one or two cinemas and cafes, but the gaiety of Trinidad was absent.

One incident rather marred our stay. The engineer officer, newly joined, died of some rare stomach trouble and had to be buried on the island. The Dutch, the ship's officers and ship's company attended the funeral. There was a long march to the cemetery which, unfortunately, attracted hundreds of little coloured boys who ran in and out of the moving ranks and caused concern at the burial ceremony when one practically fell into the freshly dug grave. It is sad to leave a fellow officer in a remote foreign island and it must be even more heartbreaking to wife or mother living thousands of miles away.

A very noticeable difference in Curacao, compared to other West Indian islands, is the poor physique of the Negro population. It was sometime before I heard the story.

During the height of the slave traffic, Curacao had been the main distributing point in the West Indies. Planters from all the islands would come to Curacao to buy their slaves. As a result, the strong Negros—male and female—left the island and those of poor physique—the "bad buys"—remained.

My last trip with *Black Bear*, before moving again, proved a memorable one. We were given orders one night to leave Port of Spain and carry out an anti U-boat patrol between Trinidad and Tobago. It was a coal-black night, moonless and starless. I was on watch with another officer. We had just passed through the Bocas, the string of islands lying across the Bay, and had increased speed to about 12 knots. We were keeping a sharp lookout, particularly for the small schooners which work the inter-island trade and as often as not sail without lights.

Suddenly out of the darkness I saw one bearing down on us. "Hard a starboard!" I yelled down to the helmsman.

We began to swing. I prayed for a quicker turn. For minutes it seemed the two of us were rushing toward each other, then very gradually we began to swing away, but then I saw—with horror— the schooner swinging in the same direction. I could hear screams and yells coming from the schooner's deck. With a horrible rending crash, we were into her. We struck the boom first, bringing down part of her mainsail, then cleanly cut off her overhanging stern with our knife-like bows. We hove to and turned on the searchlight to discover the damage. The noise from the schooner by now was as if all hell had been let loose. The animals, which they transport on board, pigs, hens, and goats were sending up a cacophony of sound. In addition to this, the coloured passengers were praying to God and shouting, "We'es drownin' man," all in one breath. We sent our whaler across with the 1st Lieutenant in charge, but he wisely did not go alongside. If he had, the whaler would have been swamped by the schooner's terrified mob. The whaler, however did pick up the helmsman who had been knocked into the water by the impact. Fortunately, he was alive, though appeared to be suffering from shock and an injured leg. The whaler's report was damage, but no one killed and no water being made.

We then began to draw alongside ourselves. At that moment I heard a coloured man scream in the stern of the schooner to another man in the bows.

"Let go de ancho' man!"

Then a voice from the bows: "Dere's no 'tring on de ancho!"

Next a voice from the stern: "Let go de damn ancho'—'tring 'or no 'tring!"

The sound of a loud splash followed. It was amusing even in the midst of all the flurry and panic. As we came alongside, men, women, children, pigs, goats, and hens poured on in seemingly unlimited numbers. We took the schooner in tow and brought her back to Port of Spain.

The Court of Inquiry revealed a certain amount of blame on both sides, but it seemed to be agreed that as the schooner's sidelights were unlit, or at least not visible, the blame was not entirely ours. The episode was a one-day sensation for Port of Spain, particularly as the daughters of two big local businessmen had been on board the schooner at the time. The girls, who had been returning from a short holiday in Barbados, told us they rather enjoyed the experience and as no serious damage had been done to body or property there were no hard feelings.

As Trinidad grew more important as a convoy gathering and calling point, a manpower shortage arose in the naval offices ashore. Once more I changed jobs, this time to Fleet Mail Officer at the base *H.M.S. Benbow.* No one ashore had the slightest idea how to run a fleet mail office, nor did I. There was no one to ask either, as the previous mail officer had disappeared rather suddenly. All I found was a Chinese clerk, some empty mailbags and a heterogeneous assortment of books and ledgers. I realized it was useless to attempt to run the office by naval standards, as no one knew how they applied to a mail office. Instead, I used an ordinary common sense system of supply and receipt.

As the fleet mail officer handled all secret and confidential mail to Britain, both service and Government, I dispatched this through accredited captains of Harrison Line cargo ships which called regularly at Port of Spain. From these same captains I collected all incoming mail. Some days I would spend hours collecting mail from the ships scattered around the anchorage and often lying miles apart.

For the six months I held this job, I lived in Port of Spain and consequently made many friends among the local people. Life was very gay. Offices closed around 4:00 PM and then those who could, dashed to the nearby beach club to swim or absorb the last rays of sunshine. In the evening many would continue to the Country Club on the outskirts of town to eat, dance, and drink. The Country Club was patronized mainly by the younger people. Both men and women were generally "dressed" but it was not considered essential. The parties never got out of hand and I never saw a case of ungentlemanly drunkenness. When the American construction gangs arrived in the early summer of '41 to take over the bases newly leased to them in the Island, this changed somewhat. They were all admitted to the club but did not attend in the same spirit. They came more to drink, the men tieless and often with beach shirt hanging loosely outside their pants. If I appear a snob in saying, this spoiled the spirit of the club, it is because I know the West Indian white. The girls like to dress gaily, and it suits them. Men found it little trouble, in consequence, to slip on a bow tie or the officers their long dress whites. It increased the party atmosphere and automatically placed restraint on over indulgence.

The American invasion, as it was called, was not popular with Trinidadians. For the first time, young parties of girls who had carelessly walked round the Savannah in the cool of the evening had to remain at home. There were frequent cases of rape and it was not deemed advisable for girls, either together or alone, to venture out after dark as was their wont.

Carnival time in Trinidad is one of complete madness. The madness affects old and young, coloured and white alike. Husbands and wives are not considered divorce-bent if they are seen with another woman or man. The coloured people are the chief noisemakers. With drums and tins they go shouting and dancing through the streets. Mock bamboo fights, with the natives dressed in weird animal costumes also take place.

To say that no one is ever hurt during carnival time would be wrong. Every year some of the older natives die with dancing fatigue—a disease not listed in any medical volume, I'm sure. From far and wide, teams of Calypso singers would compete with each other in Port of Spain at the carnival competitions. The tune is invariably the same but each competitor has his own words—always topical. There are masks and dances at the Country Club and in private homes. To watch 100 gaily dressed men and women weaving in and out of lantern-lit Country Club gardens in a conga chain is something unforgettable to we more prosaic British. It is only considered an enjoyable evening if one finishes up with at least two or three people who were not in the original party. As Scotland has its New Year and England its Christmas Day, so Trinidad has its carnival.

By now I knew Port of Spain well from its ritzy hotel life to its red light district. The latter was not greatly in evidence but not hard to find either. Coloured prostitutes walked the streets at night and the soft spoken "dahling" could be heard any evening in the dock area. One night two of us, dressed in civilian clothes, visited one of the 'dives" of Port of Spain. The women varied from white through yellow to black and the men the same. When we entered, a large scar-faced "chucker out" faced us. We were given the once-over and allowed to pass. The room in front of us was medium sized and dotted with a few rickety beer-stained tables. An aged phonograph was grinding out a jazz tune of about 1936 vintage and a white seaman was drunkenly swaying to the erratic rhythm in the arms of a coloured girl while his friends at a nearby table passed facetious remarks.

There were about a dozen men of various colour and nationality, some with girls, sitting and drinking at the other tables. As we sat down, two girls from a group standing near the small bar in one corner of the room, came hip-swaying toward us. Both wore rather short and rather soiled print dresses and nothing below them. They smiled and sat down. One was a French girl, the other an Indian. They asked us did we wish drinks so we decided that Scotch would be less likely to tear our stomachs out. When the four drinks arrived and we gulped them over in the approved manner we knew we had been wrong. We were being watched however, so ordered another round of poison to stimulate good feeling if not good health.

The French girl talked quite a bit, the same line as I was to hear in Dakar, Casablanca, and Algiers. We danced occasionally and changed from whisky to beer which seemed less potent. Later in the evening, as the room began to thin out towards a door in the rear, we knew it was time for us to leave. As we had made it clear to the girls earlier in the evening, we were not a business proposition, the order of our going was not marred by any scene. I still had an idea the management, in particular his nibs with the face, was not the least bit friendly towards us. When he barred our path at the head of the stairs and told us not to go that way but to follow him I expected trouble. We were led down an unlit, creaky, old wooden stair case, but apart from the noise of a slight scuffle behind us, reached the street safely. I was glad we were out. Two is not much in a place like that and though my companion was a 200 lb. 6-footer, he would have had little opportunity to use it had there been trouble. We discovered more about the 'dive' we visited in the days to come and realized we had stuck our necks out quite a bit.

Among my friends in the T.R.N.V.R. was one lieutenant Lovell.

He was a man well in his fifties who had volunteered with the first of the local reserves. John Lovell still owned large cocoa estates on the island. Before the war he had the largest contract in Trinidad for the shipping of cocoa to the English chocolate firm of Cadbury. We talked a lot together, and I leaned much about the way of life in Trinidad from him.

One day he asked if I would care to spend a weekend at his estates in the country. I could only manage a day so we decided on that. He was anxious to visit the estates himself as his wife had been burdened with the whole task while he had been working in the naval offices in Port of Spain. The previous day at his home in Port of Spain, his wife had been talking to a man introduced to me as a member of the local police. I was talking to John Lovell most of the time, but in occasional lapses in conversation, I heard Mrs. Lovell asking if he, the police detective, carried a revolver and something about trouble on the estates between the Negro and Indian workers. It was only when the three of us left Port of Spain early the following morning for the estate, that Mrs. Lovell asked if I recalled their conversation. I replied that I had heard only snatches. She explained that the officer she had been speaking to had been living in the estate house as protection for her in case of trouble. There had been considerable unrest of late among the natives.

About 15 miles from Port of Spain, we branched inland and began bumping over glorified cart tracks. We stopped at one cluster of native houses and Mrs. Lovell got out to speak to her overseer—an Indian. The workers' houses were at the beginning of the estates and for several miles we passed cocoa trees on either side of the road. Quite suddenly we came to the house—beautifully set in a clearing and surrounded by short clipped grass—it resembled a well-attended English garden. The house itself was of the large bungalow type of about 7 rooms with large servant quarters to the back. Only light bamboo screens separated the rooms which were open to the earth and sky on at least two sides. I was used to this by now but to the Britisher straight from home, it probably would not seem like a house at all. More like a model house planning exhibit with the walls down. It certainly was no Edinburgh Castle. There was only one servant now—a rather aged Negro—who acted as cook, butler, and gardener. In the afternoon, Lovell showed me round the nearby part of the estate. To cover the whole of it one had to ride. The story and intricacies of cocoa growing was most interesting. In the evening we sat and chatted until I had to leave again for Port of Spain.

Two days later a very excited Mr. Lovell burst into my office.

"You're lucky to be alive, my boy!" he greeted me. "You remember that overseer my wife talked to on the way to the house? He was found in the morning in about seven different pieces. One of the most brutal, sadistic crimes here for a long time."

"Oh," I said.

"But that's not all. While we were sitting over our drinks, two or three natives somehow pinched the massive safe from the next door room, lugged it up to the hills and blew it open with dynamite. If any one of us had heard them and investigated we would all probably be in the same state as the poor overseer."

In time I heard the full story. The murder had been one of revenge and jealousy. The safe-pinching had been carried out by a small group of local "bad characters," one of them an escaped jailbird. It was this group that had been responsible for the local unrest, and I gather for the murder also. I politely but firmly refused any more invitations to week-end up country.

The war in Britain was now growing in intensity. The nightly visits of the Luftwaffe were pouring destruction and death on the heads of civilians and soldiers alike. A letter from my own parents told of the story of a land mine falling in the back garden. Fortunately it failed to explode.

I became more and more irritated with my job. Ostensibly I

was in the fighting services, yet my own mother and father, as fire-watchers, were facing destruction repeatedly while I sat in complete safety in the pleasant surroundings of a West Indian Island.

For weeks I agitated for a transfer home and to destroyers. I argued at the base that I was young and a trained officer while the job I was holding required neither qualification. Eventually, after much exchanging of signals between Admiralty and *H.M.S. Benbow*, I was told I could sail for England at the first opportunity and the punch line—would be appointed to destroyers.

Officers of Black Bear *in tropic dress.*

TO THE WEST INDIES

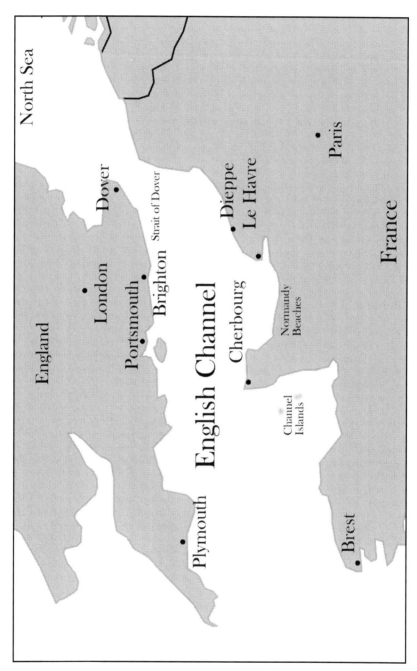

English Channel 1942, where all the encounters with German E boats and destroyers took place and for D-Day 1945.

CHAPTER 4

THE ENGLISH CHANNEL 1942

In September 1941 I said goodbye to Trinidad and boarded the new 17,000-ton luxury Royal Mail liner *S.S. Andes* for Halifax and Britain. We made the trip to Canada without escort at an average speed of 22 knots. The passengers were mostly wounded veterans of General Wavell's Army of the Nile and an odd assortment of officials and businessmen from the Far East. Among the latter was the editor of a Karachi (Pakistan) newspaper who shared a cabin with me. One evening, while sitting together in the lounge, he rather startled me by stating, "You were born in March weren't you?"

I rather dumbly nodded, unable to fathom the reason for the remark.

"Are you interested in Yogi?" he continued, "In the stars, in the future and the past?"

"If you mean, if you'll excuse the words, fortune telling, I am," I said.

It so happened I had read several books on the subject including "Cairo's," and a friend of mine in prewar days had interested me with several experiences of his own in the "unco'

67

fey" as the Scots would say.

"For the last few days," my editor friend continued, "I have been watching you." (Not difficult to understand, I thought) "and I find you a most interesting subject. Would you let me see your hand?"

I profferred the requested piece. He studied it for a while and then asked if I wished to hear his opinion. I considered I had nothing to lose, so told him all right.

For fully an hour he spoke continuously with scarce a comment from me, while my expression must have changed from one of doubt, to interest, than to amazement.

That man was no charlatan. He revealed to me the inner secrets and thoughts I considered hidden, penetrated the exterior which one shows the world, with a simplicity which made my mind and body feel naked to his probing. It is impossible to explain the latter to the reader—even to one's best friend, wife or parents. I have never failed to be accepted with the exterior I present to the world, and possibly, being something of an introvert, it is not always a true display. One's feelings towards religion, humanity, sex and personal ambition are normally one's own, in their finer details. To suddenly have them bared in front of you by a stranger is a startling experience.

In the more normal run of having one's fortune told, he was equally adept. He suggested three careers for me: medical, journalistic or the sea. The first had been thought of by my father, the second I had begun, and the third I was pursuing. I was to cross the Atlantic at least twice more, and for several years to come would travel continuously. I would marry outside my own country. I would inherit a three-figure legacy within two years. The list was very much longer, but would be pointless to enumerate. The fact that up to date, that each prediction had come true—except one—is the main point of the story. I will tell of the exception later.

When he finished, I told him how accurate he had been and asked how on earth he did it. For a minute I thought I had offended him by my rather gauche request. He appeared lost in thought for a long time, then looked at me.

"I believe you are genuinely interested," he said. "I will try to explain, but you cannot possibly hope to understand what I will tell you. It has taken me years and years to reach my present ability. In India, I studied with the Yogis in the hills for months at a time and it has not been easy."

I depend on my memory for what followed. He explained that a man's or a woman's complete physical and mental make up had to be studied first. I believe there were six classes for 1, general physical appearance, 2, color of hair, eyes and complexion, 3, shape of head, including nose, ears, chin and forehead. Those three gave the first clue. The only example I remember is a person with speckled eyes possesses a dual personality. In addition to the first three, the year, month, and date of birth had to be considered and also the lines of the hand. I recall one or two points relative to months of birth. The nearer the birth date to December the better the person by all social standards. Men born in May were weak in character, those in March, one of the most interesting and divergent types. As March is my month, I dare not say more without the embarrassing word ego occurring. I stressed the word men, because the same birth month for women is entirely different. As he pointed out to me, it must be remembered that not one of these factors can be taken singly. It is the mixture of all, plus the ability of the "reader", which gives the answer.

The most revealing statement to my mind was the fact that one holds the power over the future oneself. In other words, in reading my palm, he said, "The sign of death is the most simple to see. The sign is not in your hand, yet in another six months it might be. In the same way, the sign of impending death may already be clear in a hand, yet by following our advice death could be avoided and the sign would go."

He told me the story of a mother who brought her young son to him.

"He appeared a happy healthy boy. Suddenly, looking at his palm, I saw there clearly the sign of death. By the boy's other data, I knew his physical weakness would occur, if anywhere, in the chest. I was afraid to tell his mother, though a friend of mine, what I saw. I warned her, however, to watch for colds or any chest ailment in her son.

The family moved to Calcutta, and I lost touch with them. Eight months later that mother returned to tell me her son had died of tuberculosis three months previously. She thanked me for the warning I had given her. I felt then how much more good could have been done by telling her everything, but the large number of imposters makes us wary of speaking out."

The exception, in my case, was more a similar warning than a prediction.

"As your hand shows at present," he said "you are liable to be involved in a serious accident before you are 25—watch for it."

I was rather caustic about that one.

"With a war on I think even a "bookie" would give odds on that," I replied.

The "bookie" practically had the money in his hands several times before I was 25, but never quite collected.

My friend pledged me not to tell anyone else on the ship of our conversation. He was not a professional in the occult, but an initiate. I imagine he could have made thousands had he cared. Perhaps his knowledge had been acquired in India with a stipulation to secrecy or at least discretion. I passed many an interesting evening with him until reaching Halifax, where the number of Canadian troops jammed in the ship made private conversation impossible.

Our convoy, entirely composed of troop ships, made a quick

crossing, and on the fifth day we arrived at Liverpool. I continued to London and reported at the Admiralty. It was a pleasure to be dealt with briefly and efficiently for a change. I was sent on fourteen days leave and told further instruction would follow.

Britain in October 1941 was vastly different to Britain in 1940. In the few days I spent in London, there were continuous air raids. At home, I saw the results of the tragic surprise attack which caught Clydeside unawares. Rationing, queues and air raids were the sole topics under discussion. My leave was more a readjustment after a year's absence than a holiday. And, of course, the victims of the German air raids—civilians, women and children—a growing tragedy.

My appointment to the Hunt Class destroyer, *H.M.S. Blencathra*, November 1941, already famed for its many actions fought in the English Channel, was considered with some envy by my naval friends in Glasgow.

I will never forget my first sight of the ship. The tide was full and in the late afternoon light she lay silhouetted sleek, grey and powerful—powerful with the grace only a destroyer can convey. I could have gazed at her for hours from the quayside and those who can see beauty of line in a ship would have gazed with me. I had waited nearly two years for this moment—the moment I could set foot on a destroyer and know that I belonged there.

The formalities of meeting the captain and officers completed, I was eager to see over the ship. The gunner, an active service warrant officer, took me round. It was not a drifter or luxury yacht I saw. From the hard metal decks to the orderly row of rifles resting in their racks outside the wardroom, from the odd pieces of machinery which seemed ready to spring to life to the multitude of dials and boxes in the gunnery transmitting station, this was a fighting ship. I was very satisfied, but rather overawed by the complexity of the whole thing.

That evening after supper, the wardroom went "for a run"

HMS Blencathra.

ashore and I accompanied them. We drank beer in about five different pubs, beginning as one generally does in Portsmouth, at the Queens Hotel. As tongues became loosened I learned a lot about the ship, its work, its officers, its ratings and its achievements. *Blencathra* was the senior ship in the 1st Destroyer Flotilla comprising four ships—all Hunt class. The work was chiefly conveying the small coastal vessels east and west of Portsmouth. At present *Blencathra* was doing the rather hazardous run through the Straits of Dover to Sheerness. This involved being shelled by the heavy German batteries on Cap Gris Nes on every passage. In addition, there were German E-boats—small, fast craft carrying two torpedoes—mines which were plentiful, German aircraft, and all the natural navigational difficulties of sailing up the Thames estuary. The only menace of German naval strength, which was absent at that time, was the U-boat. In this narrow, shallow, heavily counter-mined waters of the Channel, U-boats could not operate safely.

The captain, a Commander R.N., Ruck-Keene, whom I had met, was described as the modern version of Grenville of *Revenge* fame. He looked like him—tall, gaunt, and bearded—and acted like him, even to the extent of eating the wardroom wine glasses. The first lieutenant, Tony Bloomfield, I could judge for myself as I had been talking to him most of the evening. He wore, as did the captain, the single blue and white ribbon of the Distinguished Service Cross, in those days something that spoke for itself. He acted the part of the typical playboy even to the extent of wearing a monocle. This was a "pukka" R.N. ship. I was one of only two reserve officers aboard. "Number one," as executive officers in the Royal Navy, are known, had spent his early war days on motor torpedo boats, and it was his sole desire in life, apart from debutantes, to return to them. Tony's love life, which was extensive, was shared by all on the ship. On one occasion we all helped draft a proposal of marriage in the form of a telegram to his girl-of-the-moment. This was sent on three consecutive days and three consecutive replies gave the answer "No."

I think if the answer had been "Yes" Tony would have been more surprised than anyone. The five other officers included the gunner, the engineer—a lieutenant R.N., the doctor—a lieutenant R.N.V.R.—two sub-lieutenants and one R.N.R. For a destroyer, it was a small officer complement.

Early next morning, we left Portsmouth as senior ship of a convoy bound for Bristol. Our escort duty would only take us as far as Plymouth where we would be relieved by destroyers from that base. My duties as anti-submarine control officer and in charge of confidential books, gave me little to do. I stood my watch with the first lieutenant as a "makee learn." Weather was extremely bad and the violent pitching movement of a destroyer, completely new to me, had an embarrassing effect. Fortunately I had company in my misery, even among the officers, though I was by far the worst. I managed to complete my four-hour watch on the bridge and then pretty well collapsed on the wardroom settee for the rest of the trip. The 1st lieutenant, who had recently been supplied with emergency morphine shots by the doctor, was keen to use me as a "guinea pig". I was in no mood to argue one way or the other so submitted to his needle. It did not have the slightest effect but provided much amusement to the other officers for months to come.

I had not dreamt my seasickness would have the far reaching results it did. The captain, when we arrived at Plymouth, suggested I transfer to another type of ship and appeared anxious to be rid of me. It amazed me. The only reason he gave was my sickness. Such a short-sighted, impetuous outlook is hard to believe and gave me the first clue to his irascible character. I managed to convince him, however, that it would pass and that was the last I ever heard about it. The journey back to Portsmouth was worse if anything but did not affect me at all. That one lapse was only repeated twice more in the next four years I spent at sea, and that was as much due to food and drink as ship movement.

After two days in harbour we left for our normal run through the Straits with a convoy of 15 coastal ships averaging from 500 to 1,500 tons. In this Channel run we always left Portsmouth late in the afternoon to eliminate, as far as possible, bombing attacks by German aircraft and to use the cover of darkness to run the gauntlet of the enemy's guns. I had been well-warned what to expect, and at Dungness the action alarm was sounded, and the ship company closed up to action stations.

There were only two destroyers as escorts, ourselves and the sister ship H.M.S. Fernie, commanded by the son of Admiral Sir Percy Noble, Commander in Chief Western Approaches. About two to three miles ahead of the convoy was a line of four minesweepers clearing the swept channel of any mines which might have been missed during the day or dropped by aircraft or E-boats in the early evening. We now took up station ahead of the convoy but astern of the minesweepers. *Fernie*'s station was on the starboard beam between the convoy and the German occupied French coast. My action station, as there were no U-boats in the Channel at that time, was the automatic plot—a modern self-plotting navigational instrument. During the run through the Straits, however, I navigated from the bridge chart table and clocked German fall of shot. My eyes glued to the French coast I waited for the brilliant red flash of the German guns—the second I saw it I was to start a stopwatch. It came sooner than I expected, but I did not forget the watch. Ducking under the covered bridge table, I watched the seconds tick by. At 57 I shouted to the 1st lieutenant "Now!" and he sounded the alarm bell which signaled every man on the ship to lie flat except the Captain and myself. Here I had a little run-in with the Captain who said I should get down too. I asked how could I if I am to record all of the shots? Standing on the bridge again I awaited results. A rushing roar came towards us. There were three sharp heavy explosions and three large splashes between the convoy and the English coast. Under the table again, I noted the time and "three, 1000 yards over."

I had been so excited by the rapid succession of events that I had little time to analyze my own feelings. For nearly an hour I ducked back and forth from the chart table, spotted and wrote, without paying much heed to my own inner reaction. Some of the huge 16-inch German shells passed over us with the noise and roar of an express train, others landed close before we knew it, and a few, with a distant wail, fell well astern. It is only when one had done several of these trips that the thought occurs what a shambles there would be if one shell landed. On the bridge alone and immediately below it, there were about 30 men lying closely together when a shell was in the air. One hit and there would be nothing. Occasionally the British guns would return the fire, but that seemed to spur the Germans to fresh efforts, so was unpopular with us. The Navy was more interested in jamming the German radar and thus preventing them from ranging accurately. Few ships were ever hit by the shells, yet the Germans continued using them until the Canadians finally drove them out of their gun emplacements in 1944, after the D-Day Landings.

Once past Dover, the shelling stopped. On either side of the Straits we could see the distant flashes of bomb bursts as the Luftwaffe and R.A.F. carried out their nightly missions.

Occasionally a low-flying aircraft, impossible to tell which, would roar overhead, throwing a somber shadow over the ship. The convoy rules forbade engaging enemy aircraft unless attacked. We were always afraid that some gun-happy merchant seaman might open up and bring a hornet's nest around our ears. It happened once. Those German aircraft, unable to drop their bomb load on London, would be only too delighted to find a target to complete their mission. We stole through the Channel rather like a small boy sandwiched between two adults throwing punches at each other unmercifully.

It was November 1941 and Britain was isolated and hungry for supplies. We escorted convoy after convoy through the Channel at night and safely brought them through the dangers of mines, shells and E-boats. Our engagements with E-boats were more defensive than offensive. We once had the harrowing experience of listening to the conversation of two E-boat captains through our German-speaking wireless operator.

The first report came up: "German E-boat just stated he has sighted British destroyer."

Second report came: "E-boat states he is maneuvering into position to carry out torpedo attack."

By this time we were in a near frenzy on the bridge. Our radar gave us no clue as to the enemy's position. We could not see him, yet we could hear the ominous high-pitched roar of an E-boat's engine not far away. The captain decided not to fire starshell as it would not only disclose our position but also reveal the convoy.

We waited tensely.

The last report came up: "Have fired my torpedoes."

The captain swung the ship. He did not know from where the attack was coming but evasive action might help. We waited for the jarring explosion which might follow. Minutes seemed like hours. Nothing happened. The roar of an E-boat passed very close. The yeoman grabbed the strip Lewis machine gun and dashed towards the side of the bridge. It was unfortunate that I was in his line of fire. Unfortunate for me, because he rested the gun on my tin helmet and let fly. I felt as though a woodpecker was chipping at my head for about two days afterwards. He put three quick bursts into the boat, however, and that was the last we heard of them that night. We drove them from the convoy on many occasions. We never sank one, though twice inflicted damage, but it was enough that we protected our charges, bringing their desperately needed cargoes to London.

The convoy run we featured in soon got to the ears of the press and we were given fairly widespread publicity. On several trips we carried an odd assortment of newspaper correspondents, novelists, American officers and R.A.F. pilots. The visiting officers accompanied us to observe conditions. The R.A.F. boys began to realize the difficulties of those at sea encountering aircraft.

One morning on watch, a fighter pilot and I were chatting when, suddenly, out of a low cloud, a Spitfire came roaring towards us. As he cleared our mast with a wave I heard a voice beside me say, "Bloody fool!" A convert had been made. The newspaper men were duly impressed by the dangers of the trip and vivid personal stories in the national press soon adorned our "line book." There was certainly no monotony in this type of work, if anything, there was a strain which grew with time.

At the beginning of 1942 our flotilla duties were altered. We began working up more as a fleet unit, with signal and gunnery exercises. This obviously portended something—but what? Night after night we patrolled off the French coast in the vicinity of Cap d'Antifer. Portsmouth, normally full of rumors, surpassed itself. In a naval port, security or no security, it is amazing how news gets around.

On February 1, 1942 the excitement began. The raid on Bruneval was under way. Two of our flotillas were given a patrol line some five miles north of Le Havre. We were one. No sooner had we arrived at our position than E-boats were observed on the radar screen. They were close inshore, but fortunately going toward Le Havre. Little did we know those same E-boats were looking for the landing craft waiting off shore to embark the returning paratroopers. The enemy force passed within a mile but failed to notice them. If we had engaged the E-boats, quite a different story might have been told.

At dawn the landing craft filled with tired paratroopers and commando troops sought our protection for the journey back. The weather was bad and they were all violently ill, yet we crawled along at four to six knots. How much easier it appeared to bring them on board one destroyer and dash for harbour, while the other escorted the landing craft manned by naval personnel at best speed. The B.B.C. announced the success of the raid on the one o'clock news while we were still crawling our way back only 15 miles from the French coast. Many anxious glances were cast skyward for the expected retaliatory attack from the Luftwaffe.

To our great surprise and delight it was the R.A.F. who reached us first. For the first time, from the point of view of the Channel navy, we saw a show of strength in the air which portended well for the future. More than 30 Spitfires circled us the whole way back to Portsmouth. So ended the first commando operation in Europe which owed its success not only to the valor of the troops but to the close co-operation of all three services. The end of this operation did not affect us. We still patrolled off the French coast at night, and lay at Spithead during the day. The nights of February

10 and 11th, however, we remained in harbour.

On the morning of February 12th we learned the reason for our patrols. The German battle cruisers *Scharnhorst* and *Gneisenau* and the heavy cruiser *Prince Eugene* were racing up channel from Brest to the Baltic. The bubble had burst. We were ordered out immediately, though the German ships were already past the line of Portsmouth and we would be forced into a stern chase. We never caught up, thank God, but the steady flow of signals informed us of the trend of events. Esmond's gallant squadron of six old Swordfish torpedo bombers flew right over us to engage. It has been truly said that their attack constitutes one of the finest exhibitions of self-sacrifice and devotion to duty that the war witnessed. The steady drone of R.A.F. bombers and fighters could also be heard through the low-lying clouds. A signal informed us that a flotilla of destroyers from Harwich under the command of Captain Mark Pizey, R.N., was engaging the enemy.

From a personal point of view I cannot help but be critical of the whole sequence of events. How in the first place were we supposed to engage those battleships had not fate on that one night decreed we should be in harbour? Only one of our flotillas carried torpedoes and was unavailable that day. Our small 4-inch guns and armourless sides would have been devoured by the 8 and 11-inch guns of the three German ships.

At the best, one can only say the Germans were lucky. Lucky that they first avoided the British submarines which were lying in wait for them outside Brest. Secondly, that we were off patrol. Thirdly, that neither aircraft, radar or surface ships located them till they were midway up the Channel, and fourthly, the R.A.F. was unable to attack successfully owing to the bad weather and other varied reasons. Credit is due the Germans for choosing a day when low overcast weather gave them maximum protection, but I felt this should have been accepted by those directing operations as likely and plans made accordingly. They knew the ships were going to come through fully a month before they did.

Perhaps my feelings are strong on the subject because we might have been—and the normal course of events should have been—part of the sacrifice of a seemingly costly strategy. Although the German ships got through, all three struck British-laid mines which put them out of business for some six months.

In another Channel battle, it was known through British Naval Intelligence that two German armed merchant cruisers, known as commerce raiders, were attempting to pass through the Straits of Dover to the Bay of Biscay and so to the South Atlantic. It was the job of our flotilla to intercept them, and we only awaited instructions as to which night it would be. The arrival of an additional torpedo-carrying destroyer from Harwich was fair warning that the time was near.

It had originally been intended that two destroyers of the V and W class would be added to the local force, but as luck would have it, they collided on the passage to Portsmouth and were unable to take part in the operation. This left us with four of our class—Hunts—of which only one carried torpedoes, and the Harwich destroyer. Two days later the signal arrived to proceed and carry out previous instructions. We left that night.

Dawn was approaching. In that peculiar half-light, a compromise between night and day, a faint red glow was already visible, slowly rising on the horizon. For hours it seemed we had been racing in line ahead towards the French coast—racing against the ever-gaining light.

There was a grim silence on our bridge broken only by the voice of the officer of the watch shouting a new course to the helmsman. The captain had maintained a stony silence throughout, his only movement was to glance occasionally at the chart and examine a signal. All night we had been seeking the enemy—an enemy we knew must now be somewhere near. Eyes were red-rimmed, nerves taut. The strain of peering and waiting for six long hours might yield no result. Daylight in about 30 minutes time meant failure.

The captain, at this point, asked me to order him a sherry from the wardroom. He always ordered it on a silver tray.

The captain, sipping the sherry, broke the tension. Suddenly a shout from a lookout! "Alarm Port, bearing red 20!"

My heart stopped beating. I lifted my glasses and there, sure enough, were some vague grey smudges on the horizon. The ship was springing to life. There was a note of excitement from the captain's, "That's them all right!" to the communication rating's, "Here we go, chums!"

The captain ordered "full ahead." The signal "enemy in sight" blinked down the line of ships astern. Guns were loaded and trained on the bearing—the ship was in fighting readiness.

My station was the automatic plot. As I hurried one deck below I saw with a backward glance the dots of the enemy ships with my naked eye.

I was no sooner down and saw my petty officer assistant had everything in hand than the coxswain at the wheel shouted, "Captain wants you on the bridge, sir. "

I dashed up. "Yes, Sir."

Captain orders a sherry before taking Blencathra into action.

81

"Keep an eye on the minefield to the north of us and let me know the minute we close to a mile, and stay up here until you get an idea of their disposition."

I passed the order about the minefield to my P.O. and took up my glasses again. In about two minutes their disposition was clear. The raider was surrounded by an escort of destroyers and E-boats. I counted three destroyers and about sixteen E-boats. I passed on this information to the plot.

The captain followed his "enemy in sight" signal with "going in to attack."

Enemy shells were already thudding into the water all around us. The shudder of near misses could be felt throughout the ship. The raider was using its heavier and longer-range guns to advantage. Shore batteries were adding to the support of their own ships. We were still in perfect station and as yet untouched. Not a gun had been fired from any of our flotilla—the range was too doubtful.

The German E-boats were breaking away from their charge to intercept. I told the captain we were clear of the minefield

"All right," he replied. "All right, stay here and write and let me know the radar ranges every 500 yards."

I wrote his orders, passed the ranges and watched events.

We started zigzagging and in a minute were careening through the outer ring of E-boats. They fired at us with their light armament. I saw one torpedo shave our bow, and another passed between ourselves and the next astern. I appeared to be looking into trails of red and white tracer whizzing over the bridge.

"Open Fire" shouted the captain.

Red flame spurted from all parts of every ship in the line. Shells, bullets and tracer were flying towards the enemy. The noise was deafening. It was an effort to think. Even above the noise of our own guns and the noise of the racing ship, I could hear the screeching wail of the enemy's shells passing overhead. I saw one E-boat shuddering with the concussion of pom-pom shells tearing it apart. It burst into flame and I saw the crew jumping into the water. The noise was terrific. We were engaging an enemy destroyer now at less that 200-yards range. Our shells were sweeping its decks, tearing into its vitals.

I yelled to the captain, "Range, range 2, 500 yards!"

We swung to port and the two torpedo-carrying destroyers astern now had their chance. As we turned, I saw them continue further in; saw the torpedoes leave one as it made its swing to follow us out.

Two minutes later there was a loud explosion, heard even above the noise of gunfire, and a vivid orange red spout of water.

We were still zigzagging as we engaged another enemy destroyer. At one time I thought we would collide.

At last we were clear. The enemy's gunfire was spasmodic and inaccurate. We had reformed again in line. The enemy ships had turned towards the French coast. We considered the raider had been hit all right, two E-boats probably sunk and two of the destroyers in bad shape.

The captain spoke to the yeoman of signals, "Find out what damage and casualties."

In a moment came the reply, "Some damage, slight casualties."

It seemed a miracle we had come out of that inferno so lightly.

The news of our successful action preceded us. As, still in formation, we passed the fort to Portsmouth harbour, WRENs and shore personnel were there to wave to us. The sound of our tune. "The Post Horn Gallop," which we always played entering or leaving harbour, struck a jaunty note in the still early morning air as we glided alongside. Never have I felt the glow of pride as the aftermath of successful action as much as I did that morning. To those ashore we must have appeared a brave sight. We were all torn and ripped by shell holes. The last in line had a funnel like a sieve and her whaler amidships was hanging from the davits like straggling matchwood.

Repair staffs were soon on board and casualties attended to. For the remainder of that day we slept and slept heavily.

Those days in 1942 wrought their effect on ratings and officers alike. We were always waiting for something to happen, keyed up, tense. Our morale was not failing, we were more physically and mentally exhausted. Our flotilla was always losing men. Sometimes it would be an officer from another ship and sometimes a rating. We ourselves were remarkably lucky and up to the time of my leaving, our only casualties had been two ratings with minor shrapnel wounds.

On every operation which took us close to the enemy-held coast, I had to leave all confidential and secret books at the base. I reduced this packing business to an exact science. Not once but many times I had all books off the ship within 20 minutes. On many occasions it was the last act before leaving. My well-known sacks of confidential books being dragged out was a good warning to the "lower deck" that something was afoot. I had a suspicion the captain's servant was detailed by the petty officers to pass the word if I went near the safe continaing the C.B.s (confidential books.)

The captain's favorite indication to the wardroom was, "I think I'll land my golf clubs."

The doctor's invariable reply was, "Will I stay and watch over them?"

Poor Doc had had a pretty rough trip on the occasion of our last engagement with E-boats. Normally a doctor has patiently to wait at his first aid station until someone is dragged in. There may be all hell going on outside and from within, but he has just to stay there and dream about the last pint of beer he had at some pub, or a peaceful English country lane. Our Doc was doing just that in our first aid station—the wardroom—when voices echoing down the voice pipe from the bridge attracted his attention. He left his easy chair to find out what was going on.

In his own words: "I had just put my ear to the voice pipe when the wardroom appeared to explode in my face and fly about in small pieces. When everything subsided a bit I saw that the part of the easy chair where my head had been resting was a mess of twisted spring, kapok and cloth."

Three or four 40 mm shells from an E-boat had left the wardroom a shambles and Doc's normal calm a little ruffled. It had also destroyed two of our Peter Scott watercolors and most of the wine cupboard as well as given additional views of the ocean not originally intended by the designers.

Our doctor was one of the finest men I have known. Born in Brooklyn (need I say America) he came to this country to take his medical degree; being Jewish he could not, in the 1920s, get into an American medical school. He liked it, stayed, married, and set up his own practice. He was a cheerful, happy-go-lucky man and a born mediator when tempers were on edge. Doc's imitation of two Brooklyn women in a bargain basement could stop any argument. One just had to laugh.

In the Navy, a surgeon lieutenant, particularly on a small ship, has a far more important function than doctoring. He is the one man who, if he cares, can talk to officer and rating alike, can get to the bottom of gripes and grouses and can unofficially talk to the captain. In larger ships, a padre may do this, but on a destroyer a good doctor can make a happy ship. It was our very tactful doctor who suggested the captain should go to hospital for examination. Many may not believe me when I say that our captain *did* eat wine glasses. I saw him do it on at least two occasions. This little stunt was, I believe, now playing hell with his insides and consequently his temper, (we had a few "Caine Mutiny" type incidents) and was one of the reasons for the doctor's suggestion. The first lieutenant ran the ship while the captain was away, and on his return left himself to join once again motor torpedo boats.

A fortnight later I received a little buff envelope with instructions to report to Admiralty. I was on the move again.

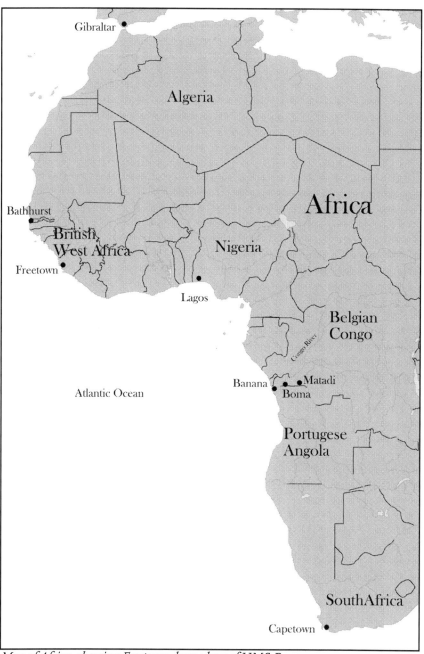

Map of Africa, showing Freetown, home base of HMS Boreas.

CHAPTER 5

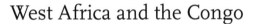

West Africa and the Congo

My six months on *Blencathra* had been worth years of experience on any other type of vessel. It had given me the knowledge and background of a destroyer officer's duties under action conditions. Though not a specialist in torpedo, gunnery, or Asdic, (anti-submarine detection), I had grasped the fundamentals. I had also qualified to take charge of a watch alone.

It was with a more firm stride I presented myself to the Commander in charge of destroyer appointments at Queen Anne's Mantions, London. It was March, 1942.

"Well Menzies, how did you like *Blencathra?*"

"Very much, Sir."

"Good. Now I'm going to send you on a series of courses, and when you're finished, give you a permanent appointment to a destroyer. You'll have about 10-days' leave to begin with—I hear some of you need it. Now go on and good luck."

"Thank you, Sir."

This was the second time I had met Commander Deneys and I was to meet him again on several occasions. He handled all officers of lieutenants' rank and below seconded to destroyers.

That man either had a photographic memory or a detailed and accurate filing system. I believe he had both. He had the confidential reports on an officer in front of him before that officer entered. He always had a cheerful word and the wonderful technique of making one feel he knew you personally. I am sure his one searching look, as you entered his office, told him everything without a word being spoken.

In the three months that followed I was "on courses." At Plymouth, it was torpedo and gunnery, and at Campbelltown, anti-submarine detection, (Asdic). The gunnery course was designed for gunnery officers in Hunt class destroyers. As I had just left a Hunt, and at times had "subbed" as a G.C.O., I found the work easy and interesting. The other two courses, torpedo and Asdic, qualified me as a control officer in either. A captain could now give me full responsibility for whichever he desired me to carry out.

In the middle of this instruction period, there was a surprising interlude. I was suddenly assigned to submarine training, and ordered to report to Campbelltown in Scotland. Well, you don't argue; you just go. So I found myself one day diving in a submarine, an old WWI, G2 sub which leaked like a sieve when a destroyer, practicing attacks, roared overhead and dropped a little 2-pound charge.

I spent a week in Campbelltown and then someone found out I was on a series of courses for a destroyer, not a submarine. Screw ups, I had already learned, are standard procedure in the Royal Navy, or for that matter, in the military everywhere. The interlude was interesting but had it continued, statistics suggest this memoir could not have been written.

At the end of June 1942 I left the Clyde in the cruiser *H.M.S. Hawkins* to join my new ship, the fleet class destroyer *H.M.S. Boreas*, based at Freetown, British West Africa. *Boreas* was not of the "Hunt" type. The name "fleet class" designates a larger, faster, torpedo type, which normally works as a screening ship for heavy fleet units. With new rapid destroyer construction, however, *Boreas*, built in 1930, was hovering between the duties of escort, (convoy work), and fleet.

The *Hawkins*, newly recommissioned, was short of specialist officers for the 14-day voyage to Freetown. I did watch on and watch off as gunnery control officer of the secondary anti-aircraft armament. I was so pleased to have a job with a definite standing that I did not mind the long hours of watchkeeping. To those who do not understand watch on and watch off, it entails four hours on duty—in my case sitting in the gunnery control director— and four hours off duty, twenty four hours a day.

The journey to Freetown, Sierra Leone, was uneventful and the return to the tropics not such a novelty to me as to many of the officers on board. Trinidad was to prove a useful background in the future.

I spent two miserable days on the dirty, rat infested, Freetown base ship, *Edinburgh Castle*, waiting for *Boreas* to return from convoy duty. When she did arrive I was pleased to see she was by far the smartest and newest destroyer in the anchorage. My arrival had been expected and I was made very welcome on board. The ship had been six months on the station and once again I had to answer the inevitable question about home. The captain, Lt. Cmdr. Jones R. N., later chatted with me in his cabin. He was interested to hear I had come from *Blencathra* and was qualified in gunnery, torpedo, and Asdic.

There were seven other officers excluding the captain. The 1st lieutenant was a very senior R.N. and the number two a junior R.N. Lieutenant Trowbridge. Both wore beards; No. 1's set was black, and rangy and No.2's red and ferocious. There were two R.N.V.R. subs both newly commissioned, an engineer lieutenant, a surgeon lieutenant R.N.V.R. and a warrant officer in charge of torpedoes. The doctor also had a beard, but the nickname of "The Goat" described its obvious sparseness. As this was a very R.N. ship, I was to be known as "the sub." In other words the senior sub-lieutenant and number three. My duties would be as Asdic and torpedo control officer. I would also stand my own watch. This now gave the ship three watchkeeping officers—the 1st lieutenant, the No. 2, and myself. That alone made my arrival popular. The two sub-lieutenants and the warrant officer served as assistants on each watch. (A warrant officer ranks between a non-commissioned officer, such as a chief petty officer, and a commissioned officer).

The approach to Freetown from the sea shows a beautiful panorama of colour—red earth, green foliage, and vivid blossom, glistening golden sand, and in the distance, purple mountains. From Tower Hill the view seaward is equally impressive. One looks over a waving sea of tropical growth and colour to the little creeks and rivers which dent and twist the shore line. Far below, the rolling breakers curl slowly over the shining sand, and the horizon stretches massive and blue into the distant Atlantic.

The town itself, with a population of 56,000, in the summer of 1942, is mostly African with a small white section. The streets are broad and clean. Grass plots and trees throw a welcome shade and coolness on the pavements. The African stores are picturesque and colourful. There are churches, chapels, and mosques of varied design: well-built banks, law courts, public offices and institutions. On the fringe of the town there is an overflow of ramshackle shops and sheds of erratic outline. The town is always full and noisy with the African traders who display their wares in bewildering profusion—mounds of rice, young green corn, bananas, ground-nuts, pieces of gaily decorated cloth, and combs from Manchester, England. The buyers and strollers make up a varied mixture of Mandrigo, Foulah, Susu, and many others, wearing coloured or plain cotton or silk gowns depending on their station.

In the evenings we stayed aboard the ship, mostly because of mosquitoes which sallied forth in greater numbers at night, but also because there was little to do. All down the West African coast entertainment is mostly a house-to-house affair and ships' personnel have little chance of entering into it. The favourite rendezvous in Freetown for us was the Lion and Palm, a two story building with a bar above and restaurant below. Mostly, however, our excursions were in the afternoons to the delightful Lumley bathing beach.

The following day I went ashore with "the wardroom" to bathe at Lumley. The naval trucks which ran at regular intervals from Freetown to the beach, drew up at the officers club. The club consisted of a large bungalow comprising a changing room, bar, and lounge. In the afternoons one could sit on the verandah or in the lounge and have the curious meal of tea, bananas, and peanuts. The peanuts and bananas were purchased from the little African boys who were always hovering in the neighborhood. The boys also acted as "caddies" for those playing golf on the nine-hole course which adjoined the club.

After five in the evening drinks were served. It was a pleasant meeting place for us all. Occasionally the club had the pleasure of a visit from the nurses stationed at one of the two local hospitals. The Army doctors, however, kept that situation well in hand. One could do little more than gaze in envy. Lumley was Freetown's saving grace as far as we were concerned. The slow Atlantic rollers bringing in their cool water were a refreshing joy to swim in. My memories of Freetown are more accurately of Lumley and consequently are more pleasant than many who have been stationed at that town.

Freetown was the base for the 21st destroyer flotilla, comprising five ships. Our work was mainly convoy, either of merchant ships or fleet units. There was more than enough to keep us busy. Traffic to Egypt was still round the Cape and thus Freetown was of vital importance as a halfway port between England and Capetown. We would take over from escorts operating from English ports just south of the latitude of Gibralter and continue either to Freetown or to 10 degrees south of the equator where the Capetown force in turn would relieve us. Independently routed ships, or those breaking off from a convoy to unload at Bathhurst, Takoradi, or Lagos were also our assignment. Those three ports handled in wartime a large amount of tonnage, mainly stores and aircraft for R.A.F. transport command ferrying across the African Continent to Egypt. Coastal Command also operated from these ports, assisting surface ships in the detection of U-boats, their equipment and supplies also had to come by sea.

West Africa played a much more important role in the war than most people realized. The Germans were not long in finding this out and for a time withdrew many of their U-boats from the North Atlantic to the West African coast. The sudden switch took a large toll of shipping for a while. It was our proud boast that we never lost a ship in convoy while working from Freetown, though many times we had the miserable task of rescuing survivors from those merchant ships sailing independently.

On my first trip on *Boreas*, while making our rendezvous with a convoy bound for Freetown, I sighted a ship's lifeboat far off on the port beam. It was the glint of the sun on the red sail which first caught my attention. I altered course and called the captain. Nothing can evoke such pity as the lonely sight of a small boat forlornly rolling in the swell in a vast expanse of ocean.

Never do you know what form of helplessness, suffering or death you are about to witness. There is not a ship will not go at its utmost speed to shorten, if only by a minute, the misery and desolation of those on board. In this case we were fortunate, the nine men were alive and strong enough to climb on board themselves. They were survivors of a Norwegian tanker and had been at sea for eight days. The one officer told us he had been heading for Freetown, and had hoped to make it only by a rough chart, and I have little doubt he would have succeeded. His calm and re-

HMS Boreas

signed statement was a wonderful tribute to the courage and determination of the men who live by the sea. Hitler, the U-boat, or anything man's now inhuman brain can devise, can never frighten or deter a seaman, be he coastal fisherman or the captain of a luxury liner, a Britisher or a Norwegian—they are the salt of the earth.

The term "stuck to the wall," a derogatory remark hurled at the personnel of "big ships" which often remain in harbour for long intervals, did not apply to *Boreas*. No sooner had we returned to port than we oiled, watered, stored, and proceeded to sea again. This time it was to convoy a single merchant ship to Bathhurst, capital of Gambia. From Bathhurst we returned to Freetown, joined a south-bound convoy as escort and broke off with two ships to Takoradi, on the Gold Coast. From there we proceeded, still with one of our charges, to Lagos. Entering the estuary to Lagos reminded me of the Thames around Richmond. On the right bank, well kept gardens, laid out with flowers, ran down to the waters' edge. The houses and churches in the background were large and dignified and at well spaced intervals. The yacht club, with its gay burgee flying, and its small 14-foot dingys lying peacefully at anchor in the little cove reminded one of a quiet English harbour scene. We anchored in midstream and spent two days visiting, sightseeing, and entertaining.

Not all of us could be wrong in giving to Lagos pride of place in the list of towns we had visited. The heat was more intense but that was my only complaint. Lagos is, of course, considerably larger that either Bathhurst, Freetown, or Takoradi. It has in fact, a larger population, (150,000), than the other three together. This was obvious by the size of the town and its more numerous and solidly-built shops and houses. The department stores—one could rightly call them so—were exactly the same as those in any British provincial town. There were movie theatres, cafes, and clubs. It was always a pleasant anticipation to be bound for Lagos and a regret to leave.

From Lagos we crossed "the line" and Neptune admitted some new members, though not without severe ritual. I can still recall the taste of the soapy shaving brush which was jammed in my mouth as I fell backwards into the jury-rigged canvas swimming pool.

At Banana, small trading and wireless station, at the mouth of the mighty river Congo, we picked up a Belgian pilot. We were bound for the Belgian town of Matadi, nearly 100 miles upstream. The Congo is no river even for a practiced seaman to negotiate himself. The current varies between 4 and 12- knots, there are deceptive shallows and abrupt twists and turns. The most unusual spectacle to watch, to all intents and purposes, a good-sized island bearing down on the ship. This is caused by large sections of the banks, as much as 30-feet across, breaking away, being caught in the current and sailing downstream. Even bushes and small

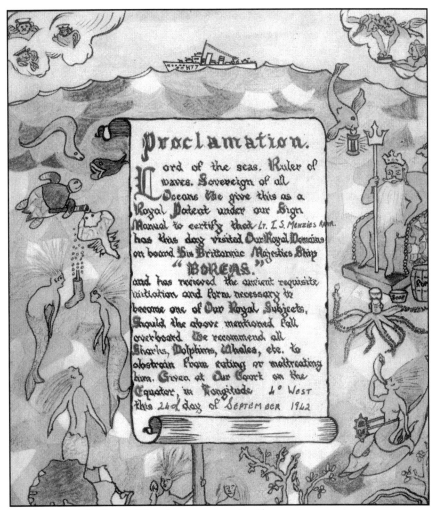

Proclamation for Ian S. Menzies, upon crossing the equator.

trees accompany the island to the sea. The journey up the Congo is really Africa as one expects to see it—dense jungle, trailing vines and steamy, marshy swamps. Occasionally a hippopotamus's beady little eyes would gaze at us from the water or a crocodile, disturbed by the ship's wash hitting the shore, would slither in its ugly, sinister way into the water.

It was a peculiar feeling, sailing up this most famous of West African rivers in one of His Majesty's ships of war. Though cargo ships of about 8,000 tons regularly called at Matadi, only one destroyer had made the trip in wartime. The fast currents make it dangerous for slow merchant ships to negotiate the river.

Moving upstream, the country on the left bank (in 1942) is Belgian, but that on the right bank, to a few miles below Matadi, is Portuguese Angola. It was here on a dry, sandy stretch of veldt that we saw a group of lions basking in the sun. From the animals to the relentless heat which beat down from overhead this was truly Africa—equatorial Africa.

Sixty miles from Banana we passed Boma, administrative centre of the district and two hours later a sharp turn in the river brought us suddenly to Matadi. The town, to me, was the biggest surprise I had seen in all my wanderings. Picturesquely situated on the side of a hill, the houses—their colours of red, blue, and white reflecting in the sun—ran in terraced series from the top to the river's edge. The green window shutters and the wooden appearance of the buildings immediately reminded me of a small Rhineland town or Swiss Alpine village. It was so strange, so sudden, yet so pleasing to the eye that my gaze of bewilderment was noticed by the Belgian pilot.

"It's pretty isn't it," he said.

The river broadened at the level of the town and provided sufficient maneuvering space. There were three freighters already alongside the wharfs, and we occupied the remaining berth. Cranes, trucks, and railway engines were all employed unloading. The scene was one of activity and efficiency combined with the wherewithal to make it so. For the remainder of that day Belgian officials visited the ship, inquired our needs, and paid their respects. The Administrator, senior official of the town also called, and invited us to dine at his home in the evening.

Many may wonder just why we were at Matadi in the first place. To explain I must retrace my steps. We had arrived at Banana with two merchant ships, which owing to their size, had been unable to proceed upstream. Both had arrived empty and were waiting to embark Belgian volunteer forces—colonial troops—for transport to Lagos and onward to North Africa. Boreas was to ferry the troops from Matadi to the waiting ships. This scheme, however, was abandoned and in its place, barges were used for transportation. The whole mission was kept "most secret." The details of loading and departure were in the hands of Belgian officials and a British Army representative.

That evening the Administrator's car arrived at the ship and the Captain, No. 1, doctor, gunner, and I made up the visiting party. The Administrator was an admirable host—tall, young, and distinguished. He spoke perfect English and amused us all by his anecdotes of the country.

Introduced to his wife, I was surprised when she said, "You are the Scot of the party aren't you? I had heard there was one. I can still say *it's a braw bricht moonlicht nicht the nicht, och I.*"

At that we both burst out laughing and I asked if she was also a Scot.

"Not quite," she replied. "You see I was born in America, but educated at Edinburgh."

The evening was made for me. Apart from the interesting sidelights of drinking Picon, a beer made from the bark of a tree, and eating my first antelope steak, the two of us reminisced of Edinburgh and Scotland for the best part of the evening.

The Administrator finally broke it up by suggesting a game.

We all sat in a circle on the floor. He picked up a pair of scissors, held them in one hand, said a few words and passed them to the person on his right. When a player had correctly followed his movements he could retire from the game or continue playing and laugh at the confusion of those not in the "know.' It was a most informal and enjoyable evening.

The next day we invited our hosts to a cocktail party on board. Very wisely we left the choice of the other guests to their discretion. We decorated the quarterdeck with gaily-strung flags and bunting and entertained about 50 people. There are few civilians who do not enjoy visiting a naval ship and I felt our party was a success.

How or why I found myself in charge of 50 ratings the following afternoon, trundling over the single road to Leopoldville in open trucks, I do not recall. Somebody must have considered it interesting and up to a point it was. The road wound its way across gullies, spanned by narrow and frail looking bridges and along the side of sheer precipices. The country was sun-scorched, dry, and dusty. There was only an occasional tree to break the monotony. The sun beat down on us unmercifully, scarcely leaving enough air to breathe. We were all thirsty and exhausted after the first hour. Now and again, a wheel of one of the three trucks would come perilously close to the edge and my responsibility would loom large and menacing before me.

We had not gone much farther when a convoy of lorries met us head-on. There was a complete impasse. Neither could go on nor yet go back. Somebody had bungled somewhere. The officer in charge of the convoy bound for Matadi talked it over with me. I was in complete agreement that it was we who should be turned— but how? Eventually, with prolonged maneuvering and a good heave from some 60 sailors and drivers, the turn was completed and we all made our way to Matadi. It was a great relief to me when we drew alongside the ship. The only casualties were two

sailors with sunstroke and 58 with a severe thirst. I did learn something from the trip—that transportation is the Congo's greatest
problem. With a wealth of raw materials available from the inte-
rior for shipment overseas there is only one railway line and one
road to handle it.

We received quite a farewell when we left Matadi, and after
disembarking our pilot at Banana were on our way to Lagos. We
left both merchant ships there and proceeded to Freetown alone.
It had been more than a month since we left our base and to
everyone's delight, we were ordered alongside the base repair ship
to "boiler clean." If boiler trouble is to be avoided a destroyer must,
after so many hours steaming, let the fires out completely and be
given a check up and a clean out. The long steaming distances on
the West African coast and the amount of work we had to do invariably ran out boiler hours far above normal.

The six days respite from duty finished, we joined two other
destroyers to convoy the battle ship *Warspite* northwards. One day
out from Freetown we received an urgent signal from base to return at utmost speed. Chief had all three boilers working over-
time within the hour and we logged the most respectable speed of
28 knots the whole way back. Twenty-eight knots on a 12-year old
destroyer with a year's service in the tropics is quite something.
The old ship stuck her stern so deep into the sea that the water
was bubbling and splashing over the quarterdeck. The vibration
in the wardroom aft was so violent that glasses rattled their way
the length of the table of their own accord. To lie down was to
submit to a forced vibromassage.

At Freetown we oiled and watered within the hour and were
off again. We were all completely mystified by these emergency
proceedings, but the captain satisfied our curiosity. The *Empress
of Canada*, a 22,000-ton Canadian Pacific Liner had been torpedoed and sunk about 300 miles south, south-west of Freetown.
There were more than 1,000 souls on board and *Boreas*, apart

from two corvettes, had been the only ship available. The corvettes had left early that morning but with a speed of only 14 knots at best would not arrive at the scene of the sinking til the following day. It was now 10:00 AM and it was hoped we would reach the survivors before dark. The chief engineer in his own words "was sitting on the safety valve" and praying that nothing would blow up.

We were making a good speed of 30 knots and going straight towards the position of the last S.O.S. signal. Everything was made ready on board. The doctor and his sick berth attendant set up two first aid stations, one forward and one aft. The first lieutenant arranged with "Jack Dusty," (stores petty officer), and the cook, the emergency meals that might be required. Large boilers of tea were prepared and the sandwiches cut. Number 2 and I remained continuously on the bridge. Additional lookouts were placed as we drew near position.

The light was beginning to go when we spotted them. There were about 10 lifeboats and numerous rafts. They were all a little scattered but we made towards the centre, heaved over our scrambling nets, and with the aid of the loud hailer told them to come alongside.

We kept all guns manned and the Asdic operating in a continuous all round sweep. The same U-boat might still be hovering around—ready to torpedo us in turn even on our errand of mercy. The captain instructed me to count survivors.

There was one officer stationed at each scrambling net, and ratings standing by to give a helping hand to those coming on board. I made a continuous circle of the ship inquiring latest figures from each officer. The decks were becoming more and more crowded. Those who had been on rafts were covered from head to foot in fuel oil—a survivor's greatest enemy. Many had been horribly gashed by barracuda and sharks. As I moved about I realized I was listening to many languages—not one of them English. The boats were crowded with men and women. The British sailor is adamant that women be the first to be brought on board. This was not always the case in the overcrowded lifeboats but "Jack" just pushed them all back till the women were passed to the front.

Many had sustained injuries when leaving the *Empress* and it was slow work hoisting them on board. One woman far gone in pregnancy was gently handled by two hefty seamen. By this time I had reported 823 survivors to the captain. The ship had already developed a unmistakable sluggish roll—the sluggish roll that has no buoyancy. The captain took one more final look from the ship. There appeared to be no boats or rafts occupied in the vicinity.

"That's all we can take anyway," he said. "The corvettes can make a final search in the morning. Give the first lieutenant a hand to settle them down."

Number 1 gave me some idea of the situation. He had brought all our own seamen—180 on deck. There had been 300 Italian prisoners of war on the *Empress*. Most of them were on board, and he had packed them into the crews' quarters forward. I went down there and found them standing shoulder to shoulder. They were still covered head to foot in oil. The air was terrible and the men so tightly jammed that they could not even sit. There was nothing could be done. The situation was the same everywhere. Cabins, mess decks, and even the engine room had its full quota. The only place "verboten" was the bridge. As I left the Italian POWs, one began screaming horribly and flailing his arms around—possibly a touch of claustrophobia. The men round about gradually pushed him down to the deck and he disappeared from view. A minute later there was silence. I explained the situation to an English-speaking Italian and told him we would sort things out in the morning. He passed the word around and everyone appeared satisfied. Tea and sandwiches were made available.

In the officers' flat, 60 women had been berthed. When I arrived I found most of them quite unconcernedly stripping themselves naked and washing in the buckets of water that had been provided. The drawers of our bureaus were wide open and shirts, shorts, and shoes were being handed round with gay abandon.

I could not understand any of the women but fortunately came across two English WRENS (Women's Naval Service). They told me the women were Czechs and Poles. They were of 2 of 6 WRENS aboard among a total of some 60 women survivors.

The wardroom was filled with Greek naval officers. On deck was a weird assortment of Frenchmen, Poles, Czechs, Greeks, and British merchant seamen. In the steward's quarters aft I found an R.N. commander, some British civilians and junior naval officers. Food and hot drinks were being passed around everywhere. The task was not easy. There were over 1,000 people on board including our own ratings. One literally could not walk on deck without standing on some one. Below decks it was impossible to move. The petty officers' mess for'd had been converted into a sick bay. There were about 50 patients, men and women lying on tables, settees and the deck. Doc was attending one after another. An Italian doctor—one of the POWs—was giving him a hand. There was a large queue outside waiting admittance. Those suffering from severe barracuda and shark bites were mainly the Italians who had only been able to cling to the rafts. In a corner I heard two men moaning. I went over but found no apparent injuries. I told Doc.

"They've got internal injuries—probably been crushed by something," he told me. "I don't like the look of them."

Nearly all our petty officers were taking orders from Doc and there was nothing more could be done. The one pregnant woman had been laid in the single sick bay cot. We were proceeding to Freetown at eight knots. The captain considered any greater speed would endanger the ship. Chief, in any case, would run out of fuel if we went any faster. Over 10 hours running at maximum speed on all three boilers had reduced our fuel to the bare requirements for the return trip.

That night a severe storm burst over the ship. The sudden crash of thunder panicked the women passengers—they thought it was another torpedo explosion. Those on deck were soaked by the tropical downpour. As quickly as it began it passed.

Shortly after, while on watch on the bridge, Doc came up beside me.

"Permission to bury two bodies, Sir."

"Go ahead Doc. Have you got anyone to assist you?"

"Yes."

As I heard two dull splashes from a point below the bridge I entered the details in the log. It was a rather macabre proceeding.

In the morning we had an opportunity to survey the situation. We brought the Italian prisoners on deck and gave them buckets of water and soap. Few of them had clothes. The ship was bereft of all spare clothing. The women had taken ours and the ratings had given theirs to the other survivors. All we could manage was a small loincloth cut from rolls of canvas for each prisoner.

The upper deck was a mess of abandoned oily clothing, pieces of food and soap, kapoc lifebelts and paper. Our own ratings were endeavoring to hose down the deck. No one seemed willing to cooperate.

One of the merchant seamen spoke to me, "Look sir, let us do the job. We'll move the b............"

I looked around and saw about six of them standing there looking very determined. I told them to carry on. There were plenty of other jobs for our own ratings. I watched the merchant seamen begin to use the hoses. A group of men were sitting on deck and appeared to ignore the water splashing closer to them. The seaman who had first asked my permission shouted for them to move away. There was no response. He waited a minute and then turned the hose on them—that cleared a path quickly. The men made a good job of cleaning the ship and appeared delighted to do it. The first lieutenant asked me if I had seen a French colonel walking around with a gun. I told him I hadn't.

"Well we'd better find him quickly. He's ready to kill some man who prevented him and his wife climbing into one of the lifeboats when the ship went down. "

Gradually I was beginning to see daylight. A chance meeting with the R.N. commander who had been one of the survivors put me wise to the situation. There had been a panic when the ship was torpedoed. A mixture of at least six nationalities—mostly service men returning from the near east—had not helped things. The merchant seamen assisted by the naval personnel had endeavored to lower the boats. The excited passengers had crammed them full before they had swung free. Boats had been dropped on other boats. There had been complete confusion and many nasty scenes even when the boats were in the water. Many of the merchant seamen and naval ratings had lost their lives when the ship went down. There was now a terrific undercurrent of feeling. This explained the action of the seamen a little while back.

Fortunately we made Freetown late that night without any incidents. Within an hour of our arrival all the survivors had left the ship. A large camp with hospital had been prepared ashore for them.

It had been an experience of a most unusual character. We were left with a ship resembling a fair ground after the crowd had gone. No one on board possessed any more clothing than he stood up in. Admiralty eventually paid us for the appropriated clothing but not till three months later. We had evidently created a precedent in the annals of Whitehall and our experience became the subject of an AFO (Admiralty Fleet Order).

In effect this new AFO declared that officers and men had to be compensated for loss of clothing taken or given to survivors, among them, in our case, some 60 women, a unique occurrence at sea in WWII.

It had been rumored that we were due to return to the United Kingdom for a refit. The captain himself had unofficially corroborated this rumor. When we received sailing instructions for Gibralter everyone was in high spirits. We left in company with the destroyer *H.M.S. Antelope.* The weather was extremely bad and we were fortunate to make the trip with no other damage other than discomfort. Meals had to be eaten crouched in a corner of the wardroom. A loop of rope helped to keep one in the corner. Everything that could possibly move in the ship was lashed down. In the wardroom, chairs were stacked in one corner and encircled by rope strung from eyebolts provided for the purpose. Sometimes we subsisted on sandwiches and a cup of tea. It was impossible for the cook to keep anything on his stove—thus hot meals were out of the question. It is a miserable existence to stand a four hour watch on an empty stomach being continuously drowned by green seas crashing over the open bridge and having one's face whipped and cut by wind and rain. To move around is a major operation. Normally I would jam myself between the gyro compass and the magnetic compass, thus leaving my hands free to take an occasional bearing.

After the first hour, one is wet and cold no matter what is worn. For the remainder of the watch it advances by degrees of misery until finally the relief arrives. Only something cold to eat and the doubtful pleasure of reading against the continuous movement of the rolling, pitching ship is the reward. The only place is one's bunk and to remain in this requires such and effort that sleep is impossible. Overhead the wind wails past and the heavy seas pound and rush over the deck with clockwork regularity. This is an everyday scene in a destroyer, especially in the winter and in the North Atlantic. It is not talked about much because a sailor accepts it as the normal course of events. No worse to him that a soldier considers a slogging 12 mile route march. It is a fallacy that the Navy has one advantage over the other services of always having a clean bed and a hot meal when desired. It may be true in big ships but not in "the maids of all work." The Mess decks are sometimes swishing in water over two feet deep. The ratings have to sleep in these conditions as best they can. Clothes are wet, hammocks wet and the men wet. Add to this the misery of those seasick, and those who can eat who can only satisfy their hunger with a few cold scraps.

Never do those at sea spend a complete night in a bunk or hammock. Even in the Army, apart from actual combat, night watches are few. The same applies in the R.A.F. A mission is completed and there is an interval before the next one. All services work as hard and do their job as well. It is only that many forget being at sea in wartime is an operation in itself.

They forget because they are never told. The Navy has said it does not need publicity. The nation accepts it as its bulwark: "It is upon the Navy, under the good providence of God, that the wealth, safety and strength of the Kingdom do chiefly depend." I do not say this for the Navy; it is for Mrs. Jones's son Johnny who served two years in corvettes, destroyers or cruisers, earned his 1939-45 star, came back and said: "Well thank God it is all over."

Convoys to Russia and across the North Atlantic are tough enough without adding U-boats, bombers, mines and battleships. Spend 28 days at sea out of 30 in a destroyer. Sleep with the sea outside three feet higher than your head and a shell of metal in between. Let your imagination throw in a torpedo cleaving towards you at 60 miles an hour with 300 lbs. of high explosive in its nose, or a mine with its vicious contact horns bumping down a ship's side. Do that every minute of the day for 28 days out of 30, for months and years. Watch ships of your flotilla have their guts torn out by "tin-fish" or an 8,000 tonner disappear without a trace. That can occur in action; it can also occur just "at sea."

The question is asked, "But you must go crazy."

The answer comes: "Those born to the sea and its dangers learn to accept it; those who are thrust into it can go through hell."

See addendum for dramatic first person story of the sinking of the Empress of Canada by a woman survivor, (a member of The Women's Royal Naval Service), as told to the author and the surprising effect it had on her life thereafter.

HMS Boreas's *base is moved to Gibraltar to take part in N. Africa landings, Nov. 1943.*

CHAPTER SIX

The Turn of the Tide

It was wonderful to arrive at Gibraltar, particularly as we considered it the last call before home. How quickly our dreams were shattered. The number of ships assembled in the harbour and outside in the anchorage should have warned us. We were too ready to accept the theory that it was another convoy preparing for the run to Malta. It was no convoy—it was North Africa.

The date was the 2nd of November 1942. Gibraltar, normally a hive of activity, exceeded itself. Ammunition for battleships and cruisers was emerging from the sunken arsenals of the "Rock" and being loaded. Frigates and destroyers which were to be part of the inshore squadrons were being fitted with additional light A/A guns and splinter mats for protection. Consultations among senior officers took place daily. Confidential book officers were seldom seen without some weighted sealed sacks.

That was the evidence. No one spoke of the things they saw. Officers and ratings alike pretended to know nothing. Conversation often became difficult. The cloak of secrecy was even greater than that at Normandy.

Gib is practically surrounded by Spain. Across the bay is

Algeciras and due north the town of La Linea. Every day hundreds of Spanish workmen crossed the frontier. There were saboteurs among them, known and unknown. The rumor of "the biggest convoy yet to sail for Malta" was encouraged. As events proved, it was successful. At least surprise was achieved.

Antelope and *Boreas* became part of the 13th destroyer flotilla—the Gibraltar force.

On the night of November 5th 1942, an impressive line of destroyers crept out into the Straits. In their wake followed a mighty battle fleet of aircraft carriers, battleships and cruisers.

The famous Force H was at sea! In the inky darkness, radar brought this large force into formation. A square "U" of destroyers practically encircled the major fleet units. We were part of that screen. All night we steamed back and forth just east of the Straits. In the morning, two miles to the south, appeared the most impressive spectacle I saw throughout the war. Hundreds of merchant ships were pouring into the Mediterranean. There were ships as far as the eye could see—tankers, liners, freighters—all moving steadily eastward in long perfect lines. As we steamed westward and they east, the Navy and the Merchant Marine—British sea power—was showing its strength. Had an enemy aircraft spotted this vast assembly of ships, I am sure the pilot would have died of heart failure.

During the night of the 7th, there was some air activity over the fleet but no attack was made. Shortly before midnight we and the destroyers *Brilliant* and *Boadicea* broke off from the main force to escort the 16-inch battleship *H.M.S. Rodney* to a position 15 miles north of Mers el Kebir on the Algerian coast. From D-Day to D-plus-2 we shook and shuddered as *Rodney* hurled shoreward her mighty 16-inch salvos. The targets, French shore batteries, replied at first, but as *Rodney* moved seaward, their range fell short, and the steady work of destruction continued. I was not surprised that the batteries finally yielded. Later I saw the devastation caused by a single 16-inch shell which had landed just short of its target. An entire Arab village had been laid flat—wisely the Arabs had left immediately when the shelling had begun.

Our one opportunity for action was frustrated by an 8,000-ton British cruiser. Two French destroyers had emerged from Mers el Kebir harbour, probably with the intention of reaching Marseilles. *Rodney* sent a signal that we engage. As torpedo control officer, this offered me a long-awaited opportunity. Two tor-

Malta convoy comes under attack.

pedoes were made ready for firing. I checked the French destroyer's speed and draught from "foreign warships" and applied the former to my disc calculator. The latter indicated the depth setting for the torpedoes. We had no sooner left *Rodney*, with everyone on board prepared for a scrap, when the cruiser *Jamaica*, last seen close inshore about 12 miles distant, dashed towards the French ships firing with everything she had. I have never witnessed such rapidity of fire from heavy armament as that of *Jamaica*. To us she appeared to be belching a steady stream of flame, and flame meant shells. One destroyer was sinking in a matter of minutes, the other was back in harbour in faster time than she came out. *Rodney* recalled us back to the screen and though disappointed, we could not but admire *Jamaica*'s dashing attack.

We returned to Gib on D-plus-3 and began the job which was to occupy us for months to come—convoy. Convoy after convoy. Empty ships back to England, full ones to Gib, Oran, Algiers, Bougie and Tripoli. Day after day we were at sea, in good weather and in bad, but mostly bad. Within four hours steaming off Lands End, we would be relieved by home-based destroyers. How we prayed, that if only for one night, we could enter an English port. We tried to bribe chief to develop "boileritis" but to no avail. An engineer would rather lose his right hand than be forced to admit engine trouble.

One memorable day, however, we managed to make Plymouth. Five of the 13th destroyer flotilla had fought and battled their way through one of the worst gales of the year with a convoy from Gib. We were, as usual, awaiting the home-based destroyer reliefs. A day passed and they did not arrive, then another, and finally came the signal: "Destroyers unable to relieve owing to weather. Proceed to Plymouth to refuel."

The gale had brought its reward. With the red and white funnel markings of Gibraltar destroyers and with the ratings and officers wearing their white cap covers—never worn in Britain—we sailed into Plymouth. It was May 1943 and not one ship of our group had been home for at least 15 months. We arrived at four in the afternoon and by five there remained only a bare minimum of men on each ship. Before eight in the evening there was not a hotel, pub, or restaurant that did not know that some of the "Med" destroyers were in port.

Plymouth opened its doors to us that night, and we in our turn walked in armed with a red brush. The entire wardroom but one, the duty officer, slept at the Hotel Continental. I say we slept, it would be more accurate to say we paid for beds. The manageress was wonderful. I recall us all eating supper with her in the kitchens at 2 AM. From two till four we held a party in the 1st

Lieutenant's bedroom. At five we sank into clean comfortable beds which neither pitched nor rolled. Breakfast at seven next morning, and two hours later I was standing on watch on the bridge, jammed in my favorite spot, being lashed by seas pounding over the open bridge; wet and cold, and returning to Gibraltar.

Our convoy duties continued unabated. We lost the one and only ship of two years' continuous duty in a run to Oran. The line of merchant ships were forming up to enter harbour. I was watching the nearest one, the *Arthur Milton*. Suddenly there was a vivid red flash, a loud explosion, and a large dark cloud of blackish matter floating overhead. Where a 10,000-ton American liberty ship had been there was nothing—nothing but a log of wood and three men clinging to it. We picked them up. Apart from shock, Doc found them uninjured. How they had survived was a mystery. They told us there had been four men on the poop deck having their hair cut at the time. One of the three men had been in the "chair", the other two waiting their turn. Of the fourth man—the barber— there was no trace. The ship had been loaded with ammunition. The Italian submarine, as we learned later, had sneaked in a lucky long range shot. Although she herself was sunk some weeks later with survivors recounting the sinking of the Liberty Ship, the *Arthur Milton*.

Oran and its vicinity brought more trouble to us than any other part of the Mediterranean. Three destroyers, of which we were one, were escorting the submarine depot ship *Maidstone* to Algiers. The disposition was one ahead, one off the port beam and one on the starboard beam. As we were nearest the shore, on the starboard beam, we were detailed to proceed to Oran, pick up a merchant ship, and return. While we were away, the destroyer on the seaward side of the convoy, the port beam was to take our station. We returned to the convoy to discover our relief had been torpedoed in our absence and was now limping into Oran harbour. Call it fate or call it luck, it still makes one think.

113

The Italian islands of Pantellaria and Lampedusa had surrendered. The British 8th Army "Desert Rats" had smashed and chased the German and Italian armies from the east while the American Armies had been battling in a pincer movement from the west.

We were lying at the time in Algiers. It was not our first visit to this city made famous in film by Charles Boyer. It truly is a French city, and an exciting and picturesque city, but I would not go much further than that. The famous Casbah of Algiers, so named after a 16th century Moorish fortress, in those 1920 years was a dangerous place. Tourists talk glibly of visiting the Casbah, but it's a cleaned up, supervised version now I'm told. It was a French officer who took us there one day. Military troops were forbidden to enter the maze of houses and alleys which compose it. As I wrote then, "one climbs innumerable steps, narrow and worn and dirty to a height of some 300 feet before entering the citadel. Shabby houses, leaning crazily towards each other, pock-marked walls and old wooden doors with small iron grills are passed on either side. The fetid smell of rotting refuse twitches the nose. Small stalls which sell a heterogeneous assortment of goods line the path and dirty beggars shuffle past. It is at night, however, that the Casbah really comes into its own. No stranger is safe in those evil smelling dark alleyways. It is a haven of prostitutes and murderers. The labyrinth of the Casbah allows criminals to hide in safety. Stabbings are an everyday occurrence. Disease is rife. Homes which were once beautiful in design and noble of occupancy now carry the red-painted sign of the brothel.

"The Casbah is something which should not be glamorized but exposed," said our guide.

On July 8th, we left Algiers with sailing instructions to join a convoy for Malta. When the sealed orders were opened we learned it was more than just a convoy. We were escorting the Second Armoured Division to Sicily. On D-Day we deployed to the western tip of Sicily. In broad daylight the entire convoy headed direct for the shore. It was a feint move to further confuse the enemy and perhaps force him to hasten some of his troops to the vicinity, thus lightening the load on the American and British troops fighting for a foothold. We expected trouble, mainly in the form of enemy air attack, but the operation was completed without any interference. At night the convoy moved to the prepared landing beaches and we departed to Malta.

Our overworked boilers and engines were showing signs of discontent. Only one of the three boilers was really safe. Number one was leaking and number two popped a few tubes every time steam was raised. For a week we lay in Selima Creek, the destroyer anchorage at Malta, undergoing repairs. The Luftwaffe and Italian Aeronautica carried out nightly raids in an endeavour to break the supply lines from Malta. During that week I began to understand just what Malta had suffered in the previous years. These raids were small compared to those in 1942 yet fearsome enough to us, who had sampled the blitzes of Plymouth and Portsmouth. The island being small, the defenses concentrated round the main harbour of Valletta, the noise during a raid was terrific. One in particular, directed at the aircraft carrier *Indomitable*, lying in Grand Harbour, was a typical example.

It was around midnight when the sirens sounded. I was duty officer and sleepily made my way to the bridge and checked that guns were closed up. The sound of low flying aircraft alerted the shore batteries to action. I heard two dull crumps as bombs landed on the town. There were about 12 destroyers in Selima Creek. As three enemy aircraft flew past at a height of fifty feet, every destroyer opened fire at the shadowy silhouettes. The noise from the other ships—our own, and the shore batteries—appeared to stagger me around the bridge. Shrapnel was pattering down over the deck and bridge with the regularity of hailstones. A destroyer not fifty yards away began firing with a light 20mm oerlikin. I had to duck low as the tracer whined over my head. There was a dull plunk beside me as a piece of shrapnel as large as my fist hit the bridge. Had it landed on my tin helmet I have an idea I would have required more than aspirin to relieve the pain. A smoke screen was adding to the darkness and confusion of the night. Those on the bridge were coughing and spluttering as the acrid smell penetrated their lungs. I tried wearing a gas mask, but as I could see nothing with it on, preferred to cough and keep control of the situation.

With the choking smoke billowing and eddying round the ship, the thunder and confusion of around 500 guns firing in a four mile area, the falling shrapnel, the red tracer piercing the blackness of smoke and night, the varying high and low pitch of low flying planes, the crump of falling bombs, and the racking coughs coming from those around me, I lost all feeling that I was a person with the power to move and think. I was no longer an individual but some small object being thrown and tossed around in a noisy pit of smoke and flame. My actions were more automatic than pre-conceived.

Those who held Malta as a fortress island in the dark days of the Mediterranean war are deserving of the Empire's highest praise. The award of the George Cross to the brave little island was fully deserved. To walk round the streets of Malta, to visit the underground workshops, and to absorb the spirit of the people was to understand what the island had suffered, what their ingenuity and confidence had achieved, and what had sustained them to do both—they themselves, the Maltese—with an underlying confidence in Britain and the Royal Navy.

Temporarily patched up in the engine room, we made one more trip to Sicily as an escort and then returned to Gibraltar. On the 2nd of September we left the "Rock" for England and decommissioning. At Liverpool we paid off after a two-year commission abroad. Our final wardroom party was as sentimental as it was boisterous. There had been one or two changes on board but not enough to lose the "family" feeling. The 1st Lieutenant had left six months previously to command his own destroyer. The number 2 had taken over the 1st Lieutenant's duties and I his. The doctor and engineer had also been relieved, but there were enough other officers remaining to make nearly two years of close comradeship under varied conditions a regretful parting.

CHAPTER 7

The Terror of Tobermory

I really appreciated the three weeks leave following our return to Liverpool and the de-commissioning of *Boreas*. For the first time I returned to a Britain no longer in doubt about victory, a Britain which was only waiting for the day when the final blow would be struck against Germany.

Londoners considered the worst of the bombing over. The terror of the V.1 and the V.2 had yet to fall on England's south coast. The complete optimism of assured victory was everywhere. The hardships of clothing and food rationing were apparent, but with the war still of primary importance, the unrest and dissatisfaction which was to come was not yet in evidence.

My interview with Commander Deneys followed in much the usual pattern. With a confidential report from the Captain of *Boreas* on his desk, he asked me what I would like to do. I gathered my courage and answered, "First lieutenant of a Hunt class destroyer."

I was surprised when he replied, "That is what I had in mind for you, but you must remember there are at present over 200 lieutenants awaiting such an appointment—and of these the majority are R.N. You would probably have to wait a month or two for a 'Hunt'. What do you think about having a D.E. (destroyer escort)? There are about 50 yet to be commissioned in the States— they are lease lend jobs built for us in American yards. There is going to be a big job for them. I personally think they are every bit as good as an appointment to a destroyer."

I had heard quite a bit about the D.E.s, or frigates, as they were known in Britain. I was sent on first lieutenants' courses for the next eight weeks. Gunnery at Whale Island, with Lt. Troubridge, the First Lieutenant of *Boreas*, in the same group. A refresher Asdic (sonar) course at Campbelltown, the newly instigated Damage Control, at London, and the Anti-Submarine Tactical School at Liverpool completed the "round." The latter course, which dealt with the latest secret tactics, weapons, and personnel of U-boats, was the most fascinating and instructive course that I had done throughout the war.

At the Liverpool Anti-U-Boat Tactical School, one large room was given over to the "game." At a distance of four feet from the walls a screen with peep-hole facilities sized for about 20 officers closed off the large area in the centre which represented the Atlantic. Each officer commanded a miniature escort vessel and from his own particular peep-hole, his view was limited to his own ship and what he would normally see from his own bridge. Movements were conducted in the normal way by signals from the senior officer. Radar and Asdic contacts were brought by signal from the school staff to the officer when they occurred.

Captain Roberts, R.N., director of the unit, controlled the attacking U-boats. At night the peep-holes were not used, if however, a commanding officer notified "staff" that he was firing star shell he would be informed by signal of what, if anything, his illumination revealed. It was a fool proof "game" which Captain Roberts reproduced from the latest reports and tactics of Doenitz's U-boat fleet in the North Atlantic. (Karl Doenitz, or Donitz, 1891-1980, German naval officer who was chief naval commander during WWII).The course was merciless to commander and lieutenant alike. During one "game" a commander, a famous U-boat killer, was quietly but firmly admonished by our instructor for a wrong tactical move which left his destroyer torpedoed and sinking.

Captain Roberts was fed with information from all sources including Commander-in-Chief Western Approaches and Naval Intelligence. He not only knew tactics, but he knew the men who commanded the U-boats themselves. Kapitan Schmidt, poorest of the German U-boat men was his "pin-up boy." He jokingly advised us if at all possible not to sink Herr Schmidt as he was of more use alive than dead.

The acoustic and "Gnat" torpedo were already being discussed at Liverpool before the Germans first used them. To do the course not only qualified one to fight the U-boat with a full knowledge of his tricks and subterfuges but also allowed one to understand how those in undersea craft reacted to various attacks and conditions. One knew in other words, the simplest way to break their morale. In the cat and mouse game of hunted and hunter, both invisible to each other, this knowledge is essential. The escort had to anticipate every move the U-boat would make. Captain Walker, most famous U-boat killer of the war, was able to do just that. The rapid and many kills by his own ship and his group, led one to believe he could read the mind of a U-boat captain 50 fathoms below—that was perfection.

U-boat captains knew of Walker's reputation well. The story is told of one captain whose boat was sunk, but he himself rescued. After being hoisted on board the ship he asked a junior officer, "Who is the captain of this ship?" On being given the answer "Captain Walker R.N.", he was heard to say, "I thought so," and with a shrug of the shoulders walked away.

Within a week of the course ending I sailed for New York on the *Queen Elizabeth*. The great *Queen*, which I had seen being built on the River Clyde, was a special thrill to be aboard even though stripped down inside as a troop ship. But I had to work my passage. As a qualified gunnery officer I was assigned to its gun control armament for the passage to New York working regular watches with 3 other officers. There was quite a group of "navy" mostly like myself bound for frigates. It was our first visit and most were prepared to "go to town" on the few days we would have in New York before joining our ships. It is useless to endeavor to describe New York as we saw it one November afternoon. From the first sight of the tall skyline to the slow journey up the Hudson it was as impressive as film and story had made it.

Leaving the ship we were all taken by bus to New York's skyscraper hotel the Barbizon Plaza which served as a dispersal point. The Admiralty had an unwritten contract with the hotel that so many rooms of the 1,000 should be reserved for incoming officers. During the war years more than 25,000 officers passed through the hotel and stayed for periods varying from one day to two months.

I shared a room with a fleet air army pilot—Jerry Connolly— and for 10 hectic days we "did" New York. Four hours after our arrival we were at the top of the Empire State building and at 2 AM we were sitting in the Stork Club surrounded by celebrities. I have few outside impressions of New York on that first visit. Jerry and I had both been overseas for nearly two years and though we had had leave in England it was nothing compared to this. We just greedily absorbed as much of New York as we could and New York as greedily absorbed as much of the almighty dollar as we had to offer. There were no hard feelings on either side. Having since lived nearly a year in the wonder city I realized if you wish to leave with unspoiled memories the only way to do it is to make your visit short and spend your money without a backward glance.

Jerry and I did just that. Jerry has never returned to New York but I have. I have had to live the everyday life of a New Yorker and my first impression has been destroyed—Jerry will retain the wonderful first experience as the only one. Together we visited every famous New York nightclub. We did, said, and saw things that one can only do on such an occasion. It was a dream holiday— one of those hopeful promises which seldom materialize.

It had to end sometime and by a lucky coincidence when our money ran out. Apart from baggage, my possessions consisted of a train ticket to Boston, where I was to join my ship and 75 cents in cash. At Boston the 75 cents became 10 after paying a taxi fare to the local barracks. The next morning I met my captain. I had developed a severe case of laryngitis, due to a number of reasons, but though scarcely audible I was able to make it clear to the captain that a loan of $10 would allow me to eat for the next few days, which would not only be to my benefit, but probably to his as well. What sort of a husky-throated, money-borrowing moron he thought I was, I have little idea—though we often laughed over our first meeting in the months to come.

I stayed a week in Boston. It is known as the most English city in America, but if the word English were changed to Irish it would be more correct. The ship, which had been launched some months earlier, was at the Bethlehem Hingham yard some 18 miles outside Boston. The captain and I went there once. It took us about five hours to get there and about five hours to get back. We decided, as did everyone who commissioned a ship at that yard, that the only answer was to live in Hingham, close to the shipyard. Boston, its vicinity and its public utilities should be used as a training ground for Commandos—they possibly might have the stamina and sense of direction to avoid getting lost. I had neither and I inevitably got lost.

Hingham was a much brighter prospect. Around a busy little shopping centre, a residential area of houses extends for many miles. Marketing is practically all done by car as there is no entirely local bus service. A train service links Hingham with Boston.

Like a landlady's "sea view" it sounds better on paper than in practice, however. To say everyone knows everyone else in Hingham is true but the synonymous English implication is untrue that gossip and scandal make life miserable. House to house visiting is the vogue but is done with a careless informality, especially among the young people, which is alien to us. There are few fences or hedges which make the Englishman's garden his own. To get to a friend's house one crosses, say, three back yards, not gardens, and arrives.

It definitely is a community and has its own community life. As one of the first places settled by the English in the days of the Mayflower there are few families who aren't related to each other in some distant way. The Old Ship Church dates back to 1681, which is old in American history. The captain and I found "digs" in the town and daily visited the yard to watch progress on the ship.

At least every second or third day the yard held a lavish buffet cocktail party to celebrate the launching or commissioning of a new ship. We were invited to all these ceremonies and met many of the local people there. It was at one of these parties I met my wife-to-be. It started with a helpless attractive girl holding a cigarette which refused to light itself and a young officer with a match. A willingness to share the possessions of life grew from that day from casualness to permanence.

Stayner, which was to be the name of our ship, had by now five officers—the captain and I, an R.N.R. gunner, an engineer and a midshipman. For the trip to Britain we were to be given a skeleton crew of Canadian officers and ratings who would be substituted on arrival by our permanent complement. There was little we could do till the ship was completed but familiarize ourselves with its equipment and compartmentalization. The day of commissioning was drawing near. We were scheduled to become *H.M.S. Stayner* on the last day of the year 1943. Two days before the ceremony the Canadian ratings arrived and I had to work them from early morning till late at night. There was a great deal to be done and only 48 hours to do it in. We managed somehow, though I had many heart attacks before it was all over.

With so many ships being commissioned there was a great deal of healthy competition between ships to put on an impressive show for the invited guests. We were determined to outdo our sister ships but two things were against us—our crew were temporary and therefore disinterested and on the day of the ceremony the weather dropped to two degrees below zero. Our *piece de resistance* was a large cake ordered from a Boston firm, showing a replica of the ship in icing on the top. Four hours before the ceremony was due to begin the cake had not arrived as expected and the gunner S/Lt Bunney made a successful taxi dash into Boston to claim it. Our guests gallantly braved the zero weather and the ship's company rose to the occasion magnificently by voting among themselves not to wear coats, thereby presenting a

The fabled cake rescued by Sub-Lieutenant Bunney "Guns" to celebrate the launching of HMS Stayner.

much snappier appearance. The spectators numbering about 100, watched as officials "turned over" the ship from the builders to the U.S. Navy and finally to the Royal Navy in a series of short speeches. The White Ensign was then hoisted and with an ecclesiastic blessing the ship was commissioned and everyone repaired below to restore circulation with a little alcohol. The cake was a complete novelty and loudly acclaimed by all—even those who had attended a hundred similar parties gave us full marks for our individuality. We felt *Stayner* had started a cut above her fellows and determined to keep her in that place.

On the day of our trials a full gale was blowing. There were several American naval officers on board to witness final tests. During the speed trials over the measured mile, we were somewhat protected by a headland from the full force of the sea but nevertheless the ship displayed every trick in its repertoire. There was nothing one could do but hold on tight as we rolled, pitched and pirouetted through heavy seas at our maximum 24 knots. The ship survived the test but few of our crew, officers, or American guests did. The captain and I agreed that the ship had stood up to the battering well. We had been very doubtful of the seaworthiness of the American built frigates, but the trial had proved our doubts unfounded. Admittedly they rolled and pitched more than our own ships but even bucking through those heavy seas at maximum speed we had shipped very little water—they were in naval language "dry ships."

The Canadian officers had joined the day of commissioning and after a short seven day "work up" off the New England coast we sailed for Britain. Whether the Admiralty were aware of the rawness of officers and crew I do not know, but they wisely routed us south by the Azores which took us clear of any possible U-boat attack. The Canadian ratings were practically all making their first trip and after the second day of heavy weather I managed to muster only eight on deck—the remainder were "flat out" with seasickness. With the assistance of two Canadian petty officers I managed to get them all on deck and for half an hour we forced them to move around and get some fresh air. The coxswain conducted physical jerks. It was a queer sight to watch some fifty white faced ratings struggling to move their bodies around against the dragging lassitude of seasickness and pitching ship. The experiment was successful, however, and next morning there were only two unable to carry out their work.

On arrival at Londonderry the Canadians left and our own complement from Devonport Barracks joined. Three more officers also arrived. Reading over the list of arrivals with the coxswain, I realized we had a big job ahead. Of the hundred and fifty ratings few had been to sea before. The average age was 19. There were about two active service ratings in the whole ship. The coxswain had left the Navy after the last war and was himself considerably

Control Officers of HMS Stayner *and MTB's, late 1944.*

out of touch. The officers were entirely R.N.V.R. The captain, engineer and midshipmen—R.N.R. Myself, the number two, the navigator, signals officer and gunner were R.N.V.R. There was an amazing mixture among us. In peace time the Captain, Lt Cmdr. Hall, D.S.C. and bar, R.N.R., had been port officer at Zanzibar East Africa. I had been an embryo journalist. The number 2, Lt Dale, a banker. The gunner a Manchester school teacher. The navigator, S/Lt Armstrong, a civil servant. The signals officer, S/

Lt Perry on loan from the Canadian Navy a commercial artist. The engineer, Lt. Poulson, an engineer on an Antarctic whaler. The midshipman a schoolboy. I was in the curious position of being in charge of these officers yet younger than all but the midshipman and the signals officer. In war time, however, one's knowledge and experience levels the age discrepancy immediately. The officers had all done their training on the lower deck. Only the number two had served before in his present rank.

During an intensive "work-up" period at Tobermory on the

West Coast of Scotland I found myself doing part of every officer's job. My past experience was invaluable for this.

With daily exercises and instruction for both officers and crew, I was working a hard 24 hour day. The instruction by the base staff was excellent. Commodore Stevenson was in charge, and though nearly 70 years of age, was the most vigorous of all. A typical day began at 7:30 a.m. Half an hour was spent cleaning ship. Promptly at 8 AM the instructors arrived on board. The ship's company were assembled on the quarterdeck. A veteran gunner shouted "double for'ard to A gun." At the same instant he hurled fire crackers in the middle of the gathered mass. That got things moving as he desired. Half way to the fo'c's'le, (bow), his assistants threw more firecrackers into the hurrying ranks. This normally caused some confusion as the rather faint-hearted endeavored to stop. More noise from behind and the pushing of fellow ratings got the timorous to run the gauntlet. The instructional gunner would then yell, "Enemy air attack imminent." That was my cue, or any officer or rating, to sound the A/A (anti-aircraft) station alarm. After a checkup of my distribution of personnel, "depth charge stations" would be called for. After lunch ratings would be divided up into instructional classes. From 4:30 to 6 damage control stations would be exercised.

Commodore Stevenson's personal visits were held in awe by everyone. He was known throughout the Navy as the "Terror of Tobermory," or "Monkey Stevenson," as a bow to his agility. Captains trembled that their executive officers would let them down and executive officers felt the same about the ship's company.

I remember one incident where the Commodore suddenly whispered to me, "Send away the boarding party to that barge over there."

I called the gunner, and he in turn assembled his boarding

He lost his grip and splashed into the water.

party. I was very pleased when they came doubling along promptly, complete with equipment. The ship's motorboat was already alongside ready to embark them. As they were going over the side into the boat the Commodore called the Gunner, "Where is your ammunition?"

The gunner looked rather nonplussed for a minute and then answered, "It's only an exercise, Sir."

"Exercise be dammed!" came the reply. "Who ever heard of a boarding party leaving without ammunition? Get it at once!"

Guns dashed away immediately, and on his return the boarding party left.

Another stunt of the Commodore's was a mid-night raiding party! Normally there were about ten ships lying at anchor in the harbour. One ship would be detailed to provide a raiding party. The object was to test the alertness of the sentries on the other ships. Our only ship's boat was the motorboat. As the engine could not be used, paddles were substituted. We decided the number two, navigator, midshipman, and two petty officers would make up the party. Lt. Dale told me what happened when they returned. It was a moonlight night but using the shadow of several ships they arrived at the bow of a French sloop without detection. It was no easy job to climb up the 20 feet of slippery anchor cable.

The navigator and one petty officer arrived on the fo'c's'le of the sloop safely but the Midshipman who was following him could not quite make the top, lost his grip and splashed into the water. This attracted the attention of the sentry who nearly shot the whole party. They paddled into the cover of the shore and determined to lay low for a while and make another attempt, but by this time the other ships in the harbour were sweeping the anchorage with their searchlights and surprise was impossible. Our raiding party took an awful beating from the rest of the wardroom for their futile attempt and inability to return with the prized possession, another ship's log book. They cleared their good name the next night, however, when another ship's party came alongside us. Unknown to me they had formed themselves into additional sentries and when the luckless raiding party scrambled on board they were drenched with our hoses—revenge was sweet.

Sea exercises were also carried out. One of our own submarines was used for Asdic and depth charge practice. Towing targets were used for gunnery. It was a vastly different ship and ship's company which left when our "work up" was completed. A final inspection by the Commodore and a word of praise all round and we left Tobermory to take our place as a fighting unit of the Royal Navy.

An idle week was spent at Greenock in the Firth of Clyde. The visit was ostensibly to carry out certain repair and installation work but little was done. The American-built frigates were as yet nobody's baby and little attempt was made to do anything. From Greenock we were sent to Portsmouth and joined forces with my old flotilla – the 1ˢᵗ D.F. (Destroyer Flotilla). Nightly we took part in patrols in mid-channel against German E-boats—the equivalent of the American P.T. boat and British M.T.B. (Motor Torpedo Boat). The E-boats were fast, light, death-dealing little boats, carrying two torpedoes and light quick firing guns. In company with the French Hunt class destroyer *La Combattant* we had our first "blooding." Our part was a minor share in the kill but it awakened the ship's company to the fact that they were really getting into action. By radar we detected three E-boats approaching our patrol position. According to a pre-arranged plan we illuminated the targets with star shell and *La Combattant* attacked from the flank. The plan was successful and the French ship left one E-boat a burning wreck in a matter of seconds. *La Combattant*'s commanding officer was full of praise for our share in the action and after this joint success the two ships often worked together.

Returning one day from patrol, we received a signal from a destroyer captain which rather brought us down to earth again.

The signal comprised the words: "Just what are you?"

I showed it to the captain and he told me to reply: "An American built frigate. Recommend you read the papers a little more often particularly *The Times* of May 16th."

The Times of May 16th referred to the successful action in the Channel naming the ships taking part.

By the middle of May 1944 several Captain class frigates had arrived at Portsmouth, and four of us were formed into a flotilla with *Stayner* as senior ship. Alterations and additions had still to be made to the frigates and it was the nature of these which gave the first clue of what was impending. One by one we were put into dockyard hands. When our turn came, I made every endeavor to obtain as much as possible. I knew we were scheduled to have additional light 20mm oerlikons fitted and also a single barreled 40mm pom-pom and twin Bofors. I gathered from the conference the captain and I attended that there was little hope of obtaining the Bofors gun, the best of the light A/A weapons, so by various wangles concentrated on oerlikons. I managed to obtain three single oerlikon mountings and two twins and a single barreled pom-pom which was mounted in the "eyes" of the ship right forward and known as the "bow chaser." This now gave us the very respectable armament of three 3 inch guns, one 40mm pom-pom and fifteen 20mm oerlikons. We came out of the deal considerably better than the other frigates. Knowing the job ahead of us, the captain and I had had no scruples in making every endeavor to equip the ship as best we could. In addition to the installation of extra armament, we were also fitted with a coastal force radio telephone set, the most up-to-date navigational aid, "Mickey Mouse" as it was known, and radar jamming apparatus which unfortunately was never completed.

Everyone on board knew now that we were to be part of the invasion forces for the great D-Day landings but when or where they were to take place had us guessing. Our job would be cooperation with coastal forces—the motor torpedo boat flotillas. This was obvious by the nature of our exercises with the small boats and coastal force officers who accompanied us on each trip as "control officers" for the M.T.B.s. Large scale practice landing operations were also carried out on the English south coast.

On June 4th the captain warned me that there had been a certain change of plans and we were to be given an additional job originally intended for another ship. I was to expect about 20 dan buoys—sea markers, which consist of buoy, pole, and flag and weighted anchoring wire—all of which had to be assembled. Could I have them ready the same day? When the lorry arrived with the massive load of gear all the officers and petty officers pitched in to get the job done. We had not sufficient time to make a thoroughly good job of it by splicing the anchoring wire on to the mooring buoys but we improvised sufficiently well to make it a sound article.

Ships company, HMS Stayner, after sinking German U boat 671, Aug. 5, 1944.

There were no suitable davits or masthead gear for dropping the dan buoys and I finally had to decide on depth charge davits, and pray that they were sound enough to stand up to the work. I say sound enough because we had found, while using one to hoist a depth charge on board, that the welded socket of the davit had parted from the deck with the greatest of ease.

We were one of the last ships to leave Portsmouth harbour. No leave had been granted for the two days we were alongside and there was scarcely a ship in port—obviously the time was drawing near. Moving down the Solent, was like driving through Piccadily Circus or down Broadway on a Saturday night. There were ships of all shapes and sizes, and odd bits of things that never looked as if they should be in the water at all. The odd bits of things were the various parts of "Mulberry" or the artificial harbours. Troopships and L.S.T.s were crammed with men, guns, tanks, and lorries. Many of the soldiers must have been on the ships for days or even weeks. As we moved through the crowded anchorage, we got a cheer from every ship as we passed. The sound of the tune, "The Post Horn Gallop", which I had broadcast over the ship's system every time we entered or left the harbour—a memory of my days on *Blencathra*—lent a cheery little note to the scene. *Stayner* was recognized not as a particular ship but as, "The one that plays that lively little tune." The playing of that record was a fight for me the whole way through. At first the ship's company thought it a rather sissy idea, but one day the broadcast system broke down and the howls of protest which came from the lower deck proved I had won through. The wardrooms complaint was purely one of taste, and led by the captain they insisted on the "March of the Gladiators". I held out, however, and the captain, as in all things connected with the ships organization, never forced the issue.

Once clear of the Isle of Wight, we joined forces with a Trinity House light vessel carrying a large number of full sized light buoys.

Both ships carried charts with the positions marked where the buoys were to be laid. Two little ships in an empty expanse of sea were preparing to create history—preparing the way for thousands of ships and men that were to pour into France. The importance of the task did not strike me at the time. I was more interested in the ordinary seaman's job of watching that the dan buoys dropped into the water the minute the hand flag held by the navigator on the bridge was waved. As we laid the buoys the Trinity House vessel approached the spot and in her turn dropped a full sized light buoy in the same spot. Our job was to make sure of the accurate position, hers to mark that position clearly.

For six hours I remained on the quarterdeck personally supervising the dropping of each dan buoy. We completed our mission successfully. The final buoy was laid only a few miles from the French coast. It was surprising there was no sign of the Luftwaffe. They were probably being fully occupied with the Allied air forces daylight saturation bombing raids. Our work of a few hours previous marked the safe channel free from mines. To small craft "buoy hopping" their way to France it would be invaluable. The sign posts were up. The last act had been completed—the might of Allied power was ready to move.

Our emergency assignment finished, we picked up our flotilla of M.T.B.s just south of the Isle of Wight. Once again we steamed over towards the French coast. It was still light when we sighted the French headland of Barfleur. Panic must have seized the German coastal troops as they saw a British frigate and 10 motor torpedo boats calmly sailing straight towards them. When only four and a half miles away, the batteries opened up. The first shots of the coastal six-inchers screamed dangerously close overhead. In fact, a very nice straddle, made me look up to see if the top of the mast was still there. The German gunners were going to it with a will. The captain ordered, "make smoke", at the same time we commenced a zig-zag which gradually opened up the range. I was amazed at the rapid response to the order to make smoke. I had scarcely pressed the buzzer to the engine room before Chief had clouds of the thickest, dirtiest, black smoke I had ever seen, issuing from the funnel. Perhaps he saw the first few shells land. On the quarterdeck Guns added his quota from the chemical smoke makers and forward even the midshipman started the smoke cans. In a few minutes everything was blotted out, not only the French coast but parts of the ship as well. I thought if every order is carried out as well as that my worries are over. We sailed up and down on a parallel course to the shore laying down a screen between the German guns and the M.T.B.s. The shelling continued through the smoke but was inaccurate. By darkness it had stopped altogether.

It was now one minute past midnight, the date June 6th, 1944 D-Day. We took up our patrol position. We, as directing ship, had the M.T B.s in a large circle around us, an area of roughly eight miles. The "feed line" to the landing beaches was practically a direct southerly line from Portsmouth to Arromanches. On either side of this line, light German naval forces could attack the convoys. In mid-channel and close to the English coast destroyers and corvettes were prepared to beat off these attacks.

Near the French coast the job had been delegated to the frigates and the motor torpedo boats. The two nearest ports on either side of the attack line were Cherbourg and Le Harvre. Cherbourg was our responsibility and a similar force to ours was off Le Harvre. That first night we patiently awaited events. The radar operator started the ball rolling with a report of several small echoes moving up close to the French coast. The oft-rehearsed plan was put into action. The movements of the German boats were plotted. The control officer sent his instructions to the motor torpedo boats lying at strategic positions. They were sent further inshore to surprise the E-boats as they attempted to creep past us by hugging the shoreline. Everything depended on our accurate plotting of our enemy's movements and the control officer's disposition of his boats. An M.T.B.'s radar is not a long range instrument and cannot be accepted as dependable much over a mile. The minute they detected the enemy themselves they could carry out their attack as desired. Immediately if they lost contact, which we could observe from our radar screen, they were re-organized by the control officer.

We could see by radar our own boats waiting, with engines stopped, for the E-boats to get within range. The control officer passed them final orders, "E-boats bearing 365 degrees, two miles go, go, go!"

The signal was received. We knew our boats were off. In the days to come I was to hear it many times, but not this first night—the engines of the M.T.B.s bursting into life in quick succession, and the increasing roar as throttles were swiftly lifted and the quick turn onto the engaging course. In a few seconds I saw straight shafts of red and white tracer crisscrossing each other. From a distance of four miles it seemed quite picturesque as the bright lines of light struck across the darkness of night. This is not picturesque when actually in one of the boats. From the radar screen we could see exactly what was happening. Our own flotilla was roaring down on the surprised enemy, spitting out a tornado of fire. The slower, steady thump of the six-pounders, could be distinctly heard. On small boats surprise is a matter of seconds. The Germans were soon returning fire. The captains of our flotilla were all experienced men. It takes experience to handle an M.T.B. charging along at upwards of 30 knots. It takes a cool brain to think above the colossal beat of four powerful engines, above the noise of gunfire—your own and the enemy's, to ignore the shells whistling overhead and thudding into your boat, and the distracting vivid light-streams of tracer.

Those few minutes of action were the most difficult for our plotting team. From the midst of that flurry of ships as shown on the radar screen they had to pick out friend from foe if they were to give our boats any advantage. Lt. Phillip Lee R.N.V.R. was control officer on *Stayner* that first night and for many nights to come. An old M.T.B. captain himself he had the confidence of his old teammates at present under his direction and a well merited confidence it was.

The captain and I remained on the bridge when the boats went into action. As the plotting room was one deck below, the captain wore a headphone set and was supplied with information by Lee. He could then, as well as directing the ship, keep abreast of the battle situation. I had control of the main and secondary armament with a separate headphone set and the captain verbally passed information he received from the plot to me. In the days to come we changed this around. The captain left the ship in my control and I wore the headphone set while he studied the plot and supplied information to me. This scheme is undoubtedly the forerunner of future naval warfare, the "brains" of the ship will not be on the bridge but in the control room. If we ourselves were about to take part in the action, however, the captain had to take over on the bridge to allow me to handle the ship's armament. The difficulty of coming from light to darkness was overcome by wearing night glasses and the use of coloured red lights in the plotting room.

Lee reported that the E-boats had been driven back to the westward and were retiring at speed, which was exactly what we desired. The captain suggested I have a look down below at the plot and see if we ourselves could now do anything to further harry the E-boats.

I saw that, though somewhat to the northward, we could intercept the German boats as they retreated from the M.T.B.s. The captain and I were itching to get into the fight ourselves. He told me he would endeavor to intercept and I was to engage whenever I could. I listened to the radar ranges and bearings of three of the enemy boats which were drawing ever closer. At 3,000 yards, the captain suggested I fire star shell and follow with our 3-inch guns. From my experience on *Blencathra*, I would have preferred to wait till the range was less. An E-boat at speed is a hard target to hit and *Stayner* had not been designed to carry out pin-point gunnery.

I fired an arc of three starshell from B gun. The illumination showed two of the E-boats clearly at about 2,000 yards. I ordered rapid salvos and all three guns poured a heavy fire towards the Germans. A minute after I waved the gunners mate, standing just behind me and controlling the secondary armament to open fire. The ship's side was blanketed in a wall of red flame as nine oerlikons and the bow chase's pom-pom added their contributions to the general broadside.

The only return fire from one E-boat sent a string of white tracer whistling over the bridge. The "pant tearer", as we knew this type of gun by, soon stopped. The E-boats swerved away and continued on their course towards Cherbourg. We had failed to sink one, but on top of their earlier clash with the M.T.B.s they must have felt very uncomfortable. Their speed of 40 knots made a stern chase useless. We had succeeded in turning them which was all that was necessary. Another hour passed quietly and then once again radar reported echoes to the westward moving in a northerly direction. It appeared that the E-boats were trying to move seaward of us this time; move out to mid-channel and then speed eastward to crash into the convoy lanes. We watched them carefully. They were still eight miles away. Our radar was working remarkably well. It was Lee who suddenly noticed a split in the echoes. One group, probably of three, was still moving northwards but another had turned straight toward us.

"Probably up to their old game of dividing their force," he commented.

This was a situation which we could handle. Had the M.T.B.s

been alone, it would have been impossible for them to grasp the situation and one group of E-boats at least would have gotten through. We directed the main force of M.T.B.s to the northward and decided we would tackle the group ahead with two M.T.B.s to support us. The group to the northward soon made contact and another short sharp engagement ensued. They reported three E-boats, two of which had turned and were being hotly chased. The third had possibly slipped past. That was bad news.

With the two M.T.B.s about a mile astern of us on either quarter, we made full speed towards what we now realized was the main force. I had slipped down to the plot again to get a quick idea of the situation. The E-boats were about six miles away. Lt. Dale, "Tubby", was plotting at a feverish rate supplied by information from the radar operator. I heard him yell to the captain.

"There are four E-boats, range 10,000 yards." This was followed in a matter of seconds by the report in a slightly higher note.

"There are five E-boats."

Just as I left the chart room for the bridge, I heard "Tubby's" shrill screech.

"There are seven E-boats, range 5,000 yards, looks as though they are going to make a torpedo attack!"

My one thought was "curtain" after "Tubby's" last dramatic report. It was no curtain for him. He was plotting and sending up reports as though his life depended on it, which to a great extent it did. The captain and I had decided that should another chance come our way we would hold our fire until the last minute, but this was obviously something different.

It appeared as if this flotilla of E-boats were anxious to write off one destroyer, as they persisted in calling us, and thus simplify their own position. Seven E-boats forced us more to the defensive. I opened with a starshell at 4,000 yards. By the illumination we could see the boats well fanned out and coming straight towards us. I distributed the firing as much as possible, an exercise we had already tested, to prevent any of the attacking boats feeling they were being neglected.

I was too busy for the next five minutes controlling fire to realize the captain was weaving the ship around like a madman. He told me it was rather like the charge at Balaclava, though instead of cannon to the left and right, it was torpedoes. After making their attack, the E-boats made off to the northwards but were intercepted by the M.T.B.s returning from their earlier encounter. There were only three of our boats plus the one which had been stationed on our starboard quarter but once again they had been turned back by the ferocity of the attack. Another short stern chase ensued and then we reorganized our forces once again. Twice more they tried to break through and failed.

At daylight we left our patrol position and made our way back to harbour. The R.A.F. were well able to handle any venturesome E-boat which might attempt to put to sea by day.

During that first night, the M.T.B.s had fought seven actions with the E-boats. Damage had been inflicted on both sides. As we had no casualties, we were pretty sure they had had the worst of the exchanges. The one E-boat which had slipped through had done no damage. We were very, very glad.

The armies of the Allies were in France. The bridgehead had been gained, and we were proud to think that in our own small way we had battled, that they would have every chance. Had those seven E-boats got through, they could have inflicted untold damage and confusion. It was good to think that not a man or ship that could have got to France didn't because of our inability. The only feeling of all of us was voiced by one petty officer on board who remarked, "We'll really get one of those b.......tomorrow."

The only discontented men on the ship were the two gunners who had not had the opportunity to fire their guns. The morale of the ship was terrific. Captain McLaughlin R.N., commanding the coastal forces was delighted with the results.

In a terrific operation such as D-Day, it is impossible to cover the whole. Our work went quite unheralded but we knew it was important and so did the Admiralty. That I am telling the story for the first time in detail will, I hope, illustrate to many the important sidelights to the big "show."

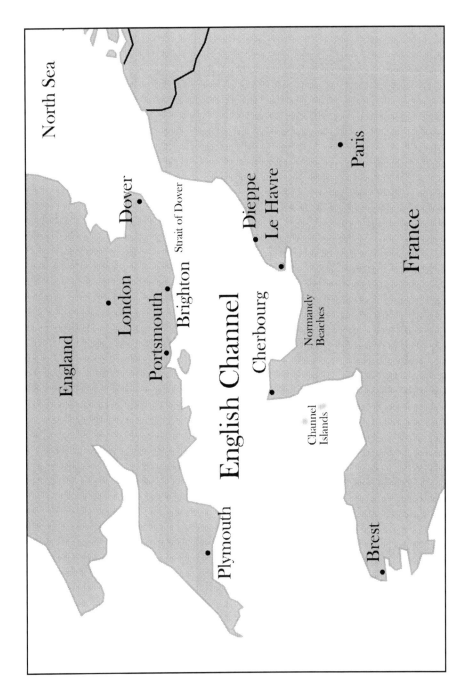

CHAPTER 8

D-Day

One of best references regarding the work of coastal forces on D-Day is contained in Gordon Holman's famous book, *Stand By To Beach*. It begins:

> "It was on D plus 9 (Thursday, June 15th), that Admiral Ramsay (Supreme Commander of Allied naval forces under General Eisenhower) told my colleague, Leslie Randall, that the Germans were bringing up their E-boats. When we first went over we caught them on the hop; he said. They were in port because they could not be out all the time on account of the strain on their crews. But now they are coming out. They come out at night and if they got through to our convoys they would cause frightful damage. Our light coastal forces and destroyers are fighting them all the time. They are simply grand. They are doing the biggest job of all."

The extract from the book continues:

> "The little ships fought as many as seven actions a night. They were hard fights, often against heavy odds and in one of them Arthur Thorpe, naval correspondent of the Exchange Telegraph Company was killed."

It was while he was with us on this self-same job that Thorpe was killed. The circumstances were much the same as when that most famous of all small ship captains, Lt Commander Robert Hitchens, D.S.O., D.S.C., was killed. Thorpe was the only man killed and by a chance shot. Fate plays funny tricks. The mention of the death of Thorpe should be a tribute to the pressmen who shared danger as much as any man serving on the ships of the Royal Navy.

Another well-known naval correspondent, A.J. McWhinnie of the *Daily Herald*, came out with us on one of our patrols. As normally happened when we had a member of the press with us, things were quieter than usual. The shelling which we underwent every night was not considered dull, by McWhinnie, however, who told the public the first news of our work in the headline: "A hundred shells in one night." Vernon Brown of the *News Chronicle* also went to sea with us on one occasion.

Not only do war correspondents risk their lives to inform the public of events, but their dispatches also boost the morale of the fighting men themselves. Nobody wishes to be a forgotten man, a forgotten ship or a forgotten army. The press in their wide coverage did much throughout the war to assist in this oft-forgotten branch of morale building. Much more could have been done but the facilities were not always available. Not until D-Day and the beginning of SHAFE (Supreme Headquarters Allied Forces Europe) did the press really begin to feel they were being given a square deal. Then it was rather late.

Beginning from that first morning of D-Day, we continued with the same job day after day. We arrived back in harbour at 9 o'clock and left again at 4. After the first successive 10 days everyone was beginning to feel the strain. Not a night passed without several engagements with the E-boats. The M.T.B.s suffered casualties, both dead and wounded. We intensified our blockade until we were practically sitting outside Cherbourg harbour. This forced us to undergo much heavier shelling from the coastal batteries, but it also gave the E-boats little room to maneuver before they were attacked. An E-boat could scarcely poke its nose outside the harbour, before M.T.B.s were racing in, bent on destruction. A typical night of shelling drew one salvo which, from the bridge, looked as though it must have landed on the quarter deck. The captain told me to call the quarterdeck and see if everything was all right. Guns answered me at the other end.

"All O.K. down there Guns?" I asked.

The reply came back, "Yes, except I'm bloody wet!"

If our radar was to be effective in picking up the E-boats we, as control ship, had to stay close inshore; if we stayed inshore we had to put up with being shelled. It was Hobson's choice.

On one famous occasion Lt John Dudley Dixon R.N.V.R., one of the most experienced of all the small boat captains, sailed to within 80 yards of the sea wall surrounding Cherbourg harbour. Came a message from John over R.T.: "Someone's turned a damned searchlight on me."

A few minutes later came his voice again, "Extinguished same searchlight with a short burst. Do you think I should land?"

John was typical of the small boat officers. There were others who worked with us—Lt Commander McCowan and Lt Mark Arnold-Foster. All had sailed with "Hitch" and were imbibed with the same fighting spirit. Among the control officers who had left their boats for this job by necessity were Phillip Lee, Christopher Dreyer, and Guy Hudson. All these officers, all R.N.V.R., had fought E-boats throughout the entire war. They knew every trick of the trade. They had suffered many casualties. They had gone back to harbour their boats riddled, their crew lying dead and wounded, and they themselves hospital cases but determinedly bringing their boats back. They had seen their fellow officers and friends buried in the little graveyard behind the base.

John Dixon himself was in hospital with a badly shot up

leg till a few days before D-Day. They tried to keep him in bed but they couldn't. He discharged himself and took over his flotilla again in time for the big show. Nearly a year later, when I was working with John in America, his leg was still giving him trouble. Phillip Lee our control officer was, as he jokingly said himself, "a mass of holes."

Those M.T.B. captains were practically all quiet, and even shy. They had probably a more intense hatred of Germans and a greater natural ability to fight at sea than any other men in the Service. It was only at their own parties that they really let themselves go.

An invitation to a "party" on board an M.T.B. required as much determination and courage as a fight with an E-boat. I have seen toughened commando officers and hardened Fleet Street journalists turn down a second invitation with a childish blush.

The hard-slugging fighting from D-Day onwards was probably their finest victory. They tore into the E-boats with a ferocity that at times appeared suicidal. On one occasion, McCowan broke through a line of E-boats at full speed, dropping depth charges and firing as he went. E-boats were rammed several times, and not by accident. Our ship had to be good, and we had to be good to have the temerity to direct men such as these.

With the fall of Cherbourg, we were switched to Le Havre and the work of blockade continued. Actions became more numerous and more intense. The Germans used heavily gunned F lighters and mine sweepers to clear a way for the E-boats. The M.T.B.s tackled these heavier units also. Many of the German boats were sunk, but we too suffered casualties. For many successive nights we became a hospital ship as well as a control ship. After an engagement, one of the boats would request permission to transfer wounded.

One has to picture first, one of those close fought actions. An M.T.B. has made a daring torpedo attack on an F lighter. She had come under concentrated fire from at least three German boats at point-blank range. The torpedo had struck its target, and the M.T.B. had moved to seaward. She had sent a message to us requesting to transfer causalities. The doctor who we carried on every trip was notified. I had arranged a rapid system of hospitalization whereby stretchers were slid on specially constructed trestles, down from the upper deck to a large seamen's mess-deck below. Here the doctor, sick birth attendant and medical party got on with their jobs.

I was standing on the deck and could hear the heavy roar of the M.T.B. drawing closer. The darkness of the night was intense. The stretcher party and I had shielded flashlights ready. When I saw the sharp flat bows of the M.T.B. about 20 yards from the ship, I flashed my light once or twice to indicate where I wanted her to come alongside. There was a slow sluggish swell. The boat rolled gently as she nosed her way alongside, her engine ticking

M.T.B.s go on patrol with HMS Stayner *as control ship, to contact German E-Boats on D-Day."*

over slowly. Ropes were thrown and she was secured alongside. In the darkness, broken only by the occasional flicker of a flashlight, it was a spectral scene.

The deck of the M.T.B. was a mess of ropes, discarded clothing and empty cartridge cases. On the deck men were lying silently. One or two seamen were talking to them—going from one to another, adjusting a blanket here a bandage there, whispering, "It's all right Bill."

The captain leaned wearily from his "dust bin cockpit." There was blood on his face. The engines were still ticking over.

"We'll take over now!" I yelled above the noise.

He answered quietly, dazedly. "O.K. We had a pretty rough time."

Our stretcher party went on board. I heard one man groan faintly as with a shattered leg he was placed on a stretcher. The men on the boat moved about slowly. They said little. Over all was the smell of exhaust fumes and burning cordite. The deck was slippery with petrol, water and blood.

The 1st lieutenant of the M.T.B. spoke to a rating, telling him to board *Stayner*. The man had a bandaged arm and his trouser leg was ripped. He was limping. He replied that he would stay, that he was all right. I asked the captain of the boat if he had been hit. He looked in bad shape. Lee had come down from the bridge and was asking him questions about the action. One more rating was brought up from the engine room. The clothing over his chest was torn. I was amazed there was so little blood. It was just a deep, raw and jagged wound. He was the last to be transferred. We hustled them all below. It had all taken just over 10 minutes. The first Lieutenant asked me if I had any more morphine as he had used his. I passed him over a complete box which I always carried.

"Just in case," he added, "thanks."

They got ready to leave again. The deck was clearer now.

Empty cartridge cases were still clanking about on the deck to each roll of the ship. The noise jangled on the nerves. The engines, which had never stopped, were revved up and the lines let go. She disappeared to be swallowed up in the darkness again—back onto patrol. That was one occasion. It happened many times.

Below decks "Doc" and his party would be working hard. If there was little likelihood of action I would try to help. I saw "Doc" work for four hours on one man, picking out pieces of shrapnel. He was bathed in sweat. To operate on a rolling ship is not part of a surgeon's training. One young seaman lay with a right leg completely shattered from the knee down. I do not know how the foot remained attached. The bone was completely shattered. He never lost consciousness, never groaned or complained. He smoked part of a cigarette and talked a little. I never heard a cry of fear or self-pity from any man brought on board. They were truly Stoic. The fate of their friends seemed more important to them than their own—it was that way on M.T.B.s.

It was annoying to us, witnessing the fights and sacrifices of the M.T.B.s that we should be contributing so little. Once or twice it was reckoned we had hit an E-boat, but as the actions always took place close to the coastline we never could prove it. If we endeavored to follow up the action it meant an intensification of coastal shelling which did not warrant the risk. Primarily we were not meant to take risks—though the word had somewhat lost its meaning—but we were to be at all times fully operative as a control ship. Therein lay our usefulness. It was disappointing but necessary. The destroyer *Forrester,* newly re-commissioned and working with us for the first time, did what we had wished to do for months. She attacked a concentration of five F lighters lying two miles off shore. We watched the whole action. The shore batteries, as expected, put up an intense barrage to protect their ships. *Forrester* was hit twice and had to put back into dry dock, where she had just come from, and she had 15 casualties.

Our opportunity to strike back occurred unexpectedly. We were on our way to our patrol position with the M.T.B.s following astern. Our Asdic was sending out its monotonous ping as usual. Admiralty had informed all ships operating in the Channel that U-boats equipped with Schnorkel might be encountered. As the instrument sent out its feeling note "ping," we heard an answering "pong" as it is described in the navy. The captain, already with two U-boats to his credit, asked me what I thought of it. It was hard to tell, there being so many wrecks in the Channel, particularly at this spot close to the English shore, but this certainly sounded better than average. We decided to investigate further.

The ship's company were closed up to depth charge stations, and the hunt began. The contact was held, and the plot reported that from the various bearings given, the "object" was moving. The M.T.B.s had been dispersed to a safe distance and instructed to cut engines.

Phillip Lee was not at all pleased with the turn of events. Not a trained U-boat hunter, he was anxious to be on the patrol position ready for E-boats. The captain and I teased him about his bored expression, but compromised with a promise to carry out one attack. If this showed results, the captain would request permission from C-in-C Portsmouth to remain; if it did not, we would carry on.

The first attack was carried out with "hedgehog" but not to the captain's entire satisfaction. It is interesting to note that he was the first man to sink a U-boat in World War II with "hedgehog." He did this while in command of the corvette *Lotus*. The evidence indicated it was a U-boat with which we were in contact. A wreck does not move against the tidal stream, nor does it take violent last minute avoiding action when an attacker approaches.

The captain sent a signal to base, "Am in contact with U-boat. Request permission to remain and investigate."

Permission was granted, much to Lee's disappointment.

U-boat hunting is an unglamorous but deadly business. In fact, for the vast majority of the ship's company it was rather "time out to watch the action." The Asdic operator, plotting team, captain, depth charge and "hedgehog" crews were fully occupied, however. There was little sign of excitement. The captain wore a headphone set over which he received information from both the plot and the Asdic team. From this data he maneuvered his ship. The time to fire was decided by the Asdic control officer. For three-and-one-half hours we dogged this contact we had never even seen. We made four "hedgehog" and six depth charge attacks. Every time the sea disrupted to the heavy explosions, we sought for evidence, but there was none forthcoming.

Another destroyer had been sent out to join us in the search, and we took turns in attacking. The hunt had started in daylight; now darkness enclosed us. The supporting destroyer had just dropped a full pattern of depth charges when suddenly there was a shout from one of the lookouts: "There's a man in the water!"

All eyes strained into the darkness of the bearing given. The searchlight was switched on and combed the surface of the sea. The shrill note from a whistle disclosed another man even closer than the first. We drew towards. He was shouting wildly in German. We exchanged congratulatory signals with a destroyer and the captain sent back a signal to Commander in Chief, Portsmouth.

"My signal******U-boat now sunk. Returning with survivors."

We picked up the engineer officer, a junior officer and a rating. They were all in an extremely nervous state though physically uninjured since they had used their escape apparatus. The other ship had picked up two survivors. The ship's company were delighted with the results. The gunner's mate was already describing the first meeting with his "oppo" on *H.M.S.*

Thornborough, a sister ship. As far as I could see, the other gunner's mate was liable to lose his 'tot' of rum and a lot of prestige with it.

At Portsmouth, the ship was inspected by the commander in chief, Admiral Sir James C. Little, who complimented the ship's company and ship's officers on sinking U-Boat 671. A two-day leave in "Pompey" (Portsmouth) was also granted—a gesture understood and appreciated.

From interrogation of the German prisoners, it was found that our first "hedgehog" attack had crippled the boat. It had been unable to surface and having no alternative, had endeavored to

Able Seaman Gripe gets into position, when we nearly crashed into the historic USS Constitution *in Boston Harbor.*

escape submerged. With the numerous attacks the boat was eventually a shambles; the only undamaged section appeared to be the control room, from where the five survivors had escaped. Now we could at least hold up our heads to the M.T.B. personnel on our own individual merit.

Painted U-boats began to appear at various points on the ship—inside the Asdic hut, on the "hedgehog" screen and on the quarterdeck. Unlike many ships, we did not discourage this practice. When a ship's company begin to feel proud of the name of their ship the battle is won. Able Seamen "Gripe" is always endeavoring to make everyone as dissatisfied as he himself. If the general morale of the ship rises, the "gripers" become mere cranks on the mess decks and no one pays any serious attention to what they say. (And, yes, we did think of those who did not escape and one never forgets. You have to live with it all of your life.)

Every day when we returned from patrol, the Captain and the control officer attended a meeting at the coastal force base. Here the doings of the previous night were discussed and policy for the future decided. The captain and control officer normally proceeded up to Portsmouth in one of the accompanying M.T.B.s the minute we reached our anchorage off Rhyde pier in the Solent. Several times we had to oil before anchoring, however, and the captain left the ship in my hands. The first time I was frankly terrified. To the captain's, "No 1, go to the oiler first, then come back and anchor—I'm going up with Lee now to the base." I simply replied, "Yes, Sir."

Guns gave me a broad wink as the captain left the bridge, and I heard the yeoman of signal mutter to his nearest neighbor, "Jimmy's going to take the ship alongside."

I could have added, "Anything may happen now."

To handle motor boats, or drifters, is one thing but to handle a 300-foot ship of approximately 1,500 tons is quite another. The layman has little idea of the damage a ship of that tonnage can do once out of control. Captain class frigates have two large anchors in the bows which protrude from the ship's side. I have seen these fearsome weapons clear another ship's deck in coming alongside with the greatest of ease. On one occasion, entering a dock in Boston harbour, I anticipated an international incident when our anchors nearly put an end to the historic old U.S. Navy Ship, Constitution. Able Seaman "Gripe" on our design of frigate, with a poor ship handling captain, was generally to be seen on the quarterdeck or fo'c'stle with his fingers jammed in his ears and a pained expression on his face on coming alongside. I am sure even the off-watch stokers came on deck that afternoon expecting some fun. I disappointed them all, and we came alongside the oiler without a bump—the only bumping was that of my knees. There must be some truth in the statement that if one can handle a variety of small boats one can handle practically anything. Lt. Cmdr. Hall was a captain who believed in training his officers and giving them confidence. I greatly appreciated what he did in allowing me to handle the ship on many occasions.

It was unfortunate that the captain should have missed our most successful action which occurred in September. No one more deserved to share it than he. A month previously he had been appointed to the office of NA.2.S.L. (in charge of R.N.R. officer appointments) at the Admiralty, and was promoted to Commander.

It was a sad parting. The day he left we moved round to the Nore command and worked from the east coast English port of Harwich. The M.T.B.s also transferred to the coastal force base there—*H.M.S. Beehive*. Patrols were mostly carried out in mid-channel and off the Belgian coast. We were still E-boat hunting but the tactical situation had changed. Convoys were now using the Scheldt estuary and E-boats were endeavoring to lay mines in the swept channels. Our greatest danger was no longer from shore batteries but from newly laid minefields. The E-boats made no attempt to engage our forces now. If they were intercepted on a mine-laying foray, they retired at high speed to harbour. Our greatest wish—to force a conclusive action—was well nigh impossible.

On the night of September 18th we were on our patrol position 23 miles northwest of Dunkirk. There were two M.T.B.s in company, stationed about a mile to the north. Radar detected three echoes moving due east. As the charted position revealed, the echoes were off the recognized convoy routes so we suspected E-boats.

It seemed too much to hope for. They seldom ventured as far across the Channel. As the line of approach was directly towards us, we patiently awaited results. The M.T.B.s were informed of the presence of suspected E-boats. Lieutenant A. V. Turner R.N.V.R., successor to Commander Hall as Captain of *Stayner*, was new to the game, having only had command of the ship for a matter of weeks, and he wisely followed the advice of the control officers. I did my best to assist him on the bridge throughout the next hour, as well as maintaining control of the armament. As usual I had gone down to the plot to get an idea of the situation. It appeared that the E-boats would first contact the M.T.B.s and therefore recognition would lie with them. The control officer agreed with me that if at all possible we should try to engage the German boats ourselves. It would also balance the odds—at present against our own force. On the bridge I briefly outlined to the captain what was going on.

"They're going in now!" the control officer shouted up "They're E-boats all right!"

We saw the familiar lines of tracer shoot across the darkness of the night, and in the background the heavy rhythmic beat of the M.T.B.s six pounder automatics. There was a heavy exchange of fire. It looked as though the three German boats were attacking fiercely. As quickly as it began, it ceased. From the plot I heard

HMS Stayner in camoulflage anchored off the Isle of Wight after night action with German E-Boats.

someone chuckle gleefully, "They've turned to the south'ard. We've got 'em!"

The control officer passed up an engaging course and we made full speed towards.

Months before, I had arranged with the radar operator that on an occasion such as this, when we were going into attack alone, he could concentrate entirely on passing ranges and bearings to me. With the compass target-bearing indicator beside me, I kept the guns trained on the approaching E-boat—according to the plot it was alone. The captain was busy with his own worries. I asked him to hold the course, as by doing so, we could give the E-boat a "copybook" broadside.

The officers at the gun mountings were repeating my ranges parrot-fashion to the guns crews. At 1,000 yards, the midshipman asked me if I had decided to board. It certainly looked that way. It was hard to describe my feelings. For months we had waited for a chance such as this. I was keyed up—determined that this time I should give the guns' crews a chance. Nothing would have made me open fire until I considered they could see the target with their naked eyes. At 500 yards I saw the E-boat. I got the target bearing indicator directly on to it. Two guns reported they had also seen it. All this happened in a matter of seconds. I gave the order to open fire.

The ship opened up in a roar of flame and noise. I saw three inch shells throw up spouts of water all round the E-boat and— what was more satisfying—ripping into the hull itself. The red streaks of oerlikon tracer converged on the dark shape like tentacles of light, tearing and destroying. I could see the small 20mm shells bouncing off. The target was obscured by the hail of fire. We had passed it now and our guns could no longer bear. One starshell was fired from X gun aft. We caught a quick glimpse of the hull of the boat lying low down in the water and fires burning.

The captain, who had been concentrating on the tactical situation and the directing of the two M.T.B.s through the control officer, was not quite sure what had happened. I told him I thought we had "written off" one E-boat. We decided to carry on and check up later. The control officer reported that he had lost contact with one of the M.T.B.s.

At that minute another action began to the north of us again. It was heavy and sustained. The captain suggested I go below and try to give him a fresh idea of the situation. The control officer was worried. It had all been fairly straightforward until this last engagement. The M.T.B. which had made the first attack had reported all O.K. She had engaged one of the E-boats at a range of about 10 yards, given it everything she had, bar the skipper's hat, and had left it stopped, burning, and abandoned.

The action we had just witnessed left us in a quandary. Which was the E-boat and which the M.T.B.? With communications broken down it was impossible to tell. One boat was coming directly toward us. We decided to fire starshell to be on the safe side. It still approached, so we followed this up with two or three rounds of H.E. It then turned away and headed towards the English coast. The one M.T.B. still in contact reported she had survivors on board and also casualties of her own. She asked permission to return to harbour, which we approved. The captain, control officer, and I, endeavoured to work out the sequence of events. There were at least four possibilities—that one of our M.T.B.s had been sunk, that one of the E-boats had been sunk, that two of the E-boats had been sunk if ours was a certainty, or that three E-boats had been sunk and the boat we had last fired on had been an M.T.B.

Base was anxious to know just what had happened. The captain informed them as best he could by signal. We proceeded to the spot where we had engaged the E-boat. It was not long before we heard the shrill blast of a whistle and lights bobbing on the water. We picked up more than 25 survivors. Many were badly "shot up." They were anything but German "supermen."

One German officer was lying on a small raft. We had put our scrambling nets over the side and the survivors were clambering up. They were then hustled aft to the large seamen's mess deck we normally used as a sick bay. While watching them climb up I noticed the German officer still lying on the raft.

One of our grizzled old three-badge able seamen—a veteran of World War I—shouted to him. "Come on 'Henie! Climb up! We ain't got all night."

The officer replied in a slow, broken German accent, "I cannot, I cannot."

Back came the reply, "Well, bloody-well try! Bloody-well try!"

He did too. He was the last to be brought on board. Immediately on deck he did not behave like a wounded man. I told the Gunners Mate to take him down aft also. Later I heard he had thrown a pocket book overboard on the way. The gunner's mate and a burly stoker who had been acting as escort had been in two minds whether to thrown him after it. As far as I could see they had put the fear of God in him. His pretence of being wounded was in order that as a German officer he would be the last to be brought on board. All the survivors were searched. One German rating lying unconscious on the mess deck "came to" to find the gunner's mate bending over him with a vicious looking hunting knife held above his chest. He tensed, cried out, and fainted again. That he feared the worst I can well believe, but the G.M.'s intentions were harmless. He was only about to cut the man's clothing to enable the sick berth attendant to dress a nasty chest wound.

In the large mess deck aft, German sailors were sitting about naked. We had ordered them to remove their oil soaked clothing in order to examine it thoroughly. I posted armed guards at the two exits from the mess deck. There was little necessity, however, as there was no fight left in those men. We had two German-speaking ratings on board who endeavoured to gather as much information as possible. In the first relief of being rescued and finding themselves alive, men talk more easily. The captain of one of the boats was on board, but as the whole lower half of his face had been shot away, we could not gather any information from him.

We were still desperately anxious to learn what the outcome of the action had been. It was not till we had practically reached Harwich that we received a signal from Dover saying the second M.T.B. had arrived there safely. It looked as though we had destroyed the entire force of E-boats. There were nearly two full crews on board us, and with survivors on the other two M.T.B.'s the evidence appeared conclusive.

At Harwich there was quite a reception committee on the

dockside to greet us. For the first time since our arrival at that port we were allowed to dock alongside—our usual berth being midstream.

As it took some time to remove the prisoners, we returned them their own, now dry, clothing. I was determined to waste as little as possible of our specially packed parcels of "survivors' clothing," on them. If the older petty officers had had their way, they would have received no food either. Five years of war make you that way. It was the young inexperienced seamen—the schoolboys of the first three years of war that brought them food— at least brought it before I was prepared to organize it. The tendency of the British, and to an even greater extent the Americans, to forgive and forget may well cost us headaches in the future.

It was soon confirmed that we had destroyed the entire force of E-boats. The ace German E-boat captain of the war—Karl Muller—was one of the survivors. He was in command of the German flotilla, and the M.T.B. captain who brought him back described him "as the most disillusioned of men." From the mass of information and reports it was concluded that we had each sunk one boat.

Admiralty communiqué number 1029 issued the following day read: "While on offensive patrol off the Belgian coast last night, the frigate *H.M.S. Stayner* (Lieutenant A.V. Turner, R.N.V.R.), in company with light coastal forces under the command of Lieutenant J.F. Humphreys, R.N.V.R., encountered a force of three E-boats in a position about 23 miles north of Dunkirk. The enemy was engaged with gunfire, and during a brisk engagement, one of the E-boats was hit repeatedly, stopped and finally sunk by *H.M.S. Stayner.* Meanwhile, the remaining two E-boats attempted to escape at speed in a north-easterly direction, but they were intercepted and engaged by M.T.B.s. During this action, which was fought at such close range that some of the M.T.B.'s guns could not be brought to bear, both E-boats were sunk. A number of survivors were picked up by *H.M.S. Stayner* and made prisoners of war. All H.M. ships returned safely to harbour, one having suffered a small number of casualties. The next of kin are being informed as soon as possible."

The press provided some excellent clippings for our "line" book which varied from" "Most Successful E-boat action of the War" to "Entire German Force Destroyed."

But there was a downside to these fierce clashes in the Channel. During November our sister ship, *Duff,* suffered 3 casualties from a mine and the next night another destroyer we worked with, *Stevenston,* had 37 casualties from a torpedo or a mine. *Stayner,* it seemed, bore a charmed life even though traveling the same mined areas as *Duff* and *Stevenston* off the Belgian coast.

Shortly after this, we were docked for refit. On my way to Glasgow on leave I was instructed to call at the Admiralty. I was interviewed by Commander Marchington R.N.V.R. who asked me if the prospect of joining a Naval Information Staff to be formed in America appealed to me. He was looking for one or two officers with a fairly wide general naval experience, including action at sea and also a journalistic background. He added that the combination appeared extremely difficult to find. If, however, I was interested, he suggested I see Commander McEachran R.N.V.R., officer in charge of the news section of the Admiralty Press Division.McEachran went more deeply into my press background, appeared satisfied, and told me that with the approval of the Chief of Naval Information, I should form part of his own party bound for New York. Meanwhile, I was to continue on leave, rejoin my ship, and I would be informed by signal of any decision reached.

This offer came as a complete surprise, and, in a sense, an honor. Why me, from among the hundreds in the Royal Navy who must have had some prior newspaper experience? The more

I thought about it, the clearer became the connecting link. It had to be my skipper, Lt. Cmdr John Hall, DSO,DSC and bar, who a month or so earlier had been reassigned to the Admiralty in charge of certain reserve officer appointments and promoted to a full commander. He and Commander Marchington worked together. John Hall knew his executive officer's background. Marchington had a spot to fill. Voila.

Later I was to learn from John Hall himself that I was being offered this media job in America or command of my own corvette. If I turned down the first choice I would get the second, but at the time I didn't know about the second choice because the US trip was too inviting both professionally and personally to turn down. I had served some five years, mostly at sea including the North African landings, Sicily, D-Day and the battles of the English Channel as well as convoys in the North Atlantic and off West Africa and between Gibraltar and Malta.

Here I must say a few words about John Hall, a first class seaman, leader and U-boat hunter, but above all a humanitarian and true friend. John hated the killing but believed in the cause.

Before being appointed to *Stayner,* John, as a lieutenant, was captain of the corvette *Lotus* one of the screening vessels in the fateful PQ 17 convoy to North Russia (Murmansk) which was decimated by German bombers and U-boats off Norway in the summer of 1942. Of 35 merchant ships loaded with millions of tons of tanks, guns, aircraft, ammunition and food, 23 were sunk. It reached disastrous proportions because after the attack began, the order was given for the convoy to disperse, leaving each merchant ship an easy target.

The escort ships were also told to scatter more or less northeastwards, but when John Hall of the corvette *Lotus* heard of ships sinking behind him, he ignored orders, turned back around and picked up survivors. John not only brought his own ship safely to Murmansk, but men who otherwise would have

Lt. Cmdr. John Hall, DSO, DSC Captain of HMS Stayner.

perished in open lifeboats and floats miles from land.

A fortnight after I had returned to *Stayner,* a signal was received that I was to be temporarily appointed to Admiralty Press Division pending embarkation for America. A trip to America was exactly what I wished, not only for the beneficial experience it would afford, but also for personal reasons. At the same time I was sorry to leave *Stayner*. I had seen her built; taken her through her teething troubles and her victories. I knew every rating on the ship personally and had shared with many their family troubles. I had watched young seamen fresh from barracks, develop into seasoned veterans. I knew the eccentricities of every gun, and the potential fighting qualities of every man. Training had been severe and discipline had been maintained on a high level—both had been necessary. As First Lieutenant (CEO) I was, as trainer and disciplinarian, in line to be somewhat unpopular. Nevertheless I left with the feeling that there was not a seaman nor officer who was not 100 percent behind the ship. I knew also that they were proud of their ship's record; one rating from a sister ship, who had disputed that point had landed in hospital. When I had needed backing up they had given it to me. In an endeavour to save a burning M.T.B. and its injured crew, I had jumped aboard to make it fast alongside. There had been no opportunity to arrange a fire fighting party; it was a case of every man thinking for himself. No sooner was I on board, however, than 10 others were beside me, the gunner's mate, popularly known as "my shadow" at my right hand. Petrol explosions shook the boat, ammunition blew up, but we remained there together, fighting the blaze with hoses until the captain finally ordered us to abandon the attempt as it appeared hopeless.

One can never forget those memories. A ship is a live, personal thing, welding men together in comradeship, in the glory of victory and in the sadness of death. I saw a tear brushed hastily away by one tough old petty officer drinking his last tot of rum with his messmates before finally leaving. Thousands of men in hundreds of ships have now left for the last time, their kit bags slung jauntily over their shoulders as they walked for the last time over the "brow." Many will never again set foot on a naval ship, but let them find an old messmate and once again all those memories will come alive and be re-lived. Leaving *Stayner* meant all those things to me.

SOMEBODY TALKED

The Bulletin

Lieutenant Ian S. Menzies.

D.S.C. Award to Reporter

Lieutenant Ian S. Menzies, R.N.V.R., a member of the reporting staff of "The Bulletin" in peace-time, has been awarded the D.S.C. for gallant and distinguished services during the period of the landing of the Allied Liberation Army in Normandy.

Lieutenant Menzies, who is 24, has been with the Navy for five years, all of the time on destroyers, and has seen much active service in various theatres of operations. In May of last year he was mentioned in despatches in recognition of his services. His home is at 68 Garscadden Road, Drumchapel, Glasgow.

Glasgow Herald, Bulletin, and Evening Times, recognize reporter.

CHAPTER 9

The American Experience

My previous years of the war had been spent at sea. Journalism was something I had left behind in an urgent, more important cause. Had I remained ashore I probably would have been more aware of the public's criticism of lack of news, of censorship and that the Services were simply inefficient at processing their various activities.

As it was, I was thrust into an organization well named "The Silent Service" but no longer in a complimentary way. Listening to the moans of newspapermen in the pubs around Fleet street I was somewhat sympathetic to their complaints of non-cooperation but I could also see the other side.

A too-rapid release of news of, for instance, a cross-English channel commando raid such as Bruneval (to capture German radar equipment) or Dieppe (to test German defenses)—in both of which we took part—can further endanger the returning troops, many of whom were in small landing craft, struggling in rough seas.

The Admiralty couldn't seem to make up its mind whether or not to send this press group to America although it did want to tell Americans that the Royal Navy was taking part in the Pacific war too, a point unknown to most Americans, as I found out.

I joined the Press Division in London in November 1944 having been informed that we would sail within a month. We finally arrived in New York on March 31, 1945 five months later. I was assigned to New York, Nicholas Monsarrat, author of "The Cruel Sea," was sent to Chicago, and our leader, a Captain Stevens, R.N.V.R., was based in Washington, DC.

It was really a sad and sorrowful story from beginning to end— too few and too late. The senior officer in the New York party was invalided out in a matter of weeks. The next senior, Lt. Cmdr Fairchild, took over, but was later sent to Chicago. That left me, a lowly lieutenant, but the only one with actual newspaper experience in sole charge of the New York group which included three WRENS (Women's Naval Service) whose mission was unclear. And no guidance or instructions came from Washington or London. And British information Service (BIS) where we were quartered, with offices in Rockefeller Center, didn't seem to have a clue as to why we were there or what we should do.

Finally, in desperation, I simply began on my own writing articles on British ships and their exploits, which were sent around to major American newspapers. For instance, knowing that the Royal Navy aircraft carrier *Illustrious* had taken part in the bombing of Japan, I would use this small news information to write a feature story on the history of the *Illustrious*, thus in the *Baltimore Sun* I would get the headline "*Illustrious*, The Most Glamorous, Fought from Malta to Shakishima."

I would also write about the return by Britain of American-built lend-lease destroyer escorts (D.E.s) and small carriers showing that Britain was observing the lend-lease return agreements. These stories also received a good press. So we did what we could and the lieutenant in charge of radio wrote some dramatic scripts, of the war at sea, which were aired over top radio stations.

And, of course, on May 8, 1945 the war in Europe was declared over which I celebrated with a joyful mass of thousands in Times Square, cheering and singing. Three months later (September 2, 1945, following the bombing of Hiroshima and Nagasaki, Japan surrendered in a famous ceremony aboard the U.S. battleship *Missouri* (known as "The Big Mo"), and on September 12 the Japanese forces in Southeast Asia ceased fighting.

The working side of my stay in America with the Royal Navy press group was somewhat depressing, but fortunately, for me, offset by personal happy events. A month after my arrival, my engagement to Barbara Newton was announced and solemnly sealed in love and marriage in "The Old Ship Church" Unitarian in Hingham, Massachusetts—a church which claims to be the oldest Meeting House in continuous service in the United States.

So life changed. Instead of looking for E-boats and U-boats, the hunt turned to apartments which in the WWII years were as scarce as hen's teeth. We, however, were reasonably lucky. We were offered, through the English Speaking Union, a one-bedroom apartment on West 57th Street, diagonally opposite Carnegie Hall, by a retired British major and his wife who escaped the city's heat for four months every spring-summer to enjoy a country cottage in upper New York State. I think, hearing of our plight, it was a war-effort gesture at a very reasonable rate.

Well, it didn't take us long to find out one reason why our landlords left for the summer; it was to escape what was known in those days as "The Jersey Invasion"—squadrons of mosquitoes blown across the Hudson River from New York's neighboring state of New Jersey. Our apartment had no cooling system, no window screens and no air conditioners. It was a choice many nights of keeping the windows closed, being bitten or inhaling DDT, which few realized at the time was poisonous.

But all good things come to an end, and mosquitoes or no mosquitoes, the apartment was a blessing. But now with fall's arrival we were on the hunt again. This time all we could get was a shared apartment with a doctor and his wife. We did have our own bedroom and bathroom, but that was it. We spent a lot of time in movie houses and restaurants.

Our landlord, Dr. Smith, a semi-retired proctologist, was friendly and helpful, even to cooking breakfast for us on Sundays. He had some attachment to the training camp of then world heavyweight boxing champion Joe Louis. Needless to say, he was a fight fan and had an amazing knowledge of the sport. He took me several times to amateur fights at the New York Athletic Club.

While I did my thing in the offices of British Information Services (BIS) including talks to outside groups, my wife kept busy too. A trained commercial artist and a graduate of Boston's Vesper George School of Art (now closed), she had found a job at Contempo studios doing fashion drawings for the media. Her real love, however, was watercolor painting which she had developed while studying, under a scholarship, with the well-known artist Henry Hensche who operated a school each summer, in those years, at Provincetown, Cape Cod.

New York is an exciting city, a blood-stirring world metropolis, especially for the career-striving young, but to me, when the chance arrived to live and work in New York, I chose Boston. I hadn't lost the challenge of competition, but five years of war at sea had broadened my visions of a fuller, more mature, satisfying life.

And contributing to that feeling was my wife's hometown of Hingham, Massachusetts, a coastal farming community of some 12,000 in the 1940s. At our marriage in the historic Old Ship Church I really did feel the cycle of time. Abraham Lincoln's ancestors had lived there and went to church there. My wife's grandfather, William Foster, was a selectman, and chairman most of the 40 years he served—a New England town record. A wonderful old gentleman who contributed to writing the history of the town, his tales of early life and political doings were fascinating. Even in the 1940s, it seemed hard to believe that the train that puffed and chugged its way from Scituate through Hingham to Boston took soldier volunteers on their first step to the American Civil War.

Hingham also was, and is, a truly beautiful little town, especially Main Street, with its then glorious elms, which Eleanor Roosevelt, spoke so highly of during a visit. And it was just such a friendly community. There were few fences separating the white-painted traditional Cape Cod, Colonial and Garrison homes. Kids ran across neighbors' yards to get where they were going without upsetting owners. There were nine small working farms in town and it seemed that every area was in a sense farm-centered with either crops or cows. Ponds were scattered around town as well, adding a picturesque tableau of scarf-wrapped skaters in winter.

I really did feel the cumulative impact of the place, and the people, an aura of peace and gentleness, particularly while sitting in the aged maple pews, each with its own little door, in the Old Ship Church.

Here I was, a Scot, in my white summer Royal Navy uniform, and my wife-to-be, a New Englander, related to Peregrine White one of the Mayflower's famed passengers. What did the forefathers of us both think of this union, or should we call it a re-union? Did their blessing go with us? We felt it did.

And as events tumbled along, we decided that as I had to return to Britain to be demobilized, Barbara would come too. She wanted to, and she knew what she wanted to do—paint. She loved Scotland, its romantic and violent history, and its crumbling old castles which she painted—the more crumbling the better. She did not complain of the ration cards, still necessary to buy food and other goods. Fortunately my parents had moved from the bustle of the city itself and from apartment living to a semi-detached home with a garden on the city's outskirts where she could

Ian and Barbara cut their wedding cake, June 16th, 1945.

walk to farms—and paint—and, as in New York, she was soon doing fashion drawings for big retail houses in Glasgow.

The Glasgow Herald, true to their promise, hired me back on my demobilization which, from a grateful government, included a suit and a hat which we chose from racks. Neither fitted. There was no GI bill, no opportunity to resume an education cut off by war and service. The worst thing, however, was in the newspaper business itself. Broadsheets, like *The Glasgow Herald*, could only print four pagers which literally was one broadsheet folded over.

I could occasionally get a feature story accepted on the editorial page which paid a little extra but competition for minimal space was enormous.

As a reporter, I did my share of covering events and because of my service in the Navy I was told I would be the paper's "Naval Correspondent" which in effect meant that I would cover the exercises of the Home Fleet, a traditional peace-time event to which the nation's larger newspapers, the BBC and press associations sent representatives. Eighteen media people were assigned to this particular four-day exercise in October, 1946 involving 48 Royal Navy ships.

I was to join the navy's most technically up-dated aircraft carrier, the 32,000-ton *Implacable*, capable of carrying 48 aircraft and with a war-time crew of 2,400, reduced post-war to 1,500.

As we sailed out of the Firth of Forth on the Scottish east coast and into the North Sea, a lively party developed between media representatives and pilots which led to my agreeing, cavalierly, to fly the next day on a bombing exercise. My pilot-to-be, I was assured by others, was the best aboard and for that matter in the entire naval air arm with 1,100 successful landings in war and peace on oft-times pitching decks.

Come the next day I signed my life away and with minimal attentiveness was tucked into the rear cockpit of a Firefly (adapted Spitfire) and was told we would carry out a dummy dive-bombing attack from 6000 feet on a target being towed by the *Implacable*.

Our flight of five Fireflies, led by my pilot, made four dives on the target and each time, as we came out of the dive, I was in doubt, as to whether I would pass out.

After the fourth dive and having ridiculously placed my handkerchief as protection over some of the menacingly protruding knobs and switches on the dashboard, I heard over the intercom: "Emergency, emergency, I need to come in."

My pilot, name unremembered, then informed me and his flight of four other planes that the emergency plane had not just landed but crashed-landed in the middle of the flight deck.

Furthermore, this was not a happy situation as we were running out of fuel (the plan was for a short exercise) and hadn't enough to reach land. So we started circling the big carrier, round and round, awaiting developments. Fortunately one arose in the form of a large bulldozer which slowly, ever so slowly from our vantage point, pushed the crashed plane overboard.

But now, I gathered, with fuel about gone, we all had to land pretty damn quick, which meant about every 30 seconds which is a bit hair-raising and leaves no allowance for error.

So my first carrier landing was not only memorable but made good copy for the Herald's new "Naval Correspondent." And my pilot could chalk up number 1,101 in his record of safe landings.

Also among unforgettable coverages, was the day I was sent to the city of Dundee to cover a speech by Churchill, yes Winston, who was heading for his second term as Prime Minister. It was a good election speech and I called the city desk.

"How much can you take?" I asked.

"One paragraph," I was told.

That did it. That said it all. The paper shortage was acute in Britain and I could see it going on for years, as it did. Barbara and I talked it over. I knew American papers had a few problems too, but nothing like Britain.

She didn't want to go back. She was truly in love with Scotland and with the countryside which ranged from pastoral to rugged and mountainous with the sea always close. But what determined our decision to go was housing. It would be years before we could buy a house to bring up a family and prices were out of sight. My parent's home, though comfortable, was too small, nor did we wish to impose for long on their hospitality.

So the decision was made. We would return to America and I would gamble that I could find a newspaper job somewhere. It seemed that we were running our own lend-lease system—me to America, Barbara to Scotland, then Ian and Barbara back to America. But you can do things like that in your mid-20s without concern. And we had the pleasure of crossing to Britain in the Great Clyde built liner, come troopship, *Queen Elizabeth*.

Curiously enough, when I was still in New York, both Barbara and I made a special trip to Boston to welcome back my old ship, *HMS Stayner*, being returned under lend-lease. Sadly, for me, she was returned to be later broken up at Hegie's yard in the Savin Hill Basin.

We hoped we would meet a more acceptable fate.

CHAPTER 10

It All Comes Together

Our return trip from Scotland to America was by Anchor line freighter. This shipping line sailed from Glasgow to New York on a regular basis carrying cargo and some 20 passengers. On our crossing, in the fall of 1947, the cargo was mostly Scotch whisky and some half dozen big Clydesdale horses whose welfare became the worry of the entire ship–I should add in addition to some concern for my wife, Barbara, who was at this time some 6 months pregnant.

Concern for the prized horses was based on the knowledge that if horses develop violent seasickness it can be fatal. For a pregnant woman a heaving ship can be dangerous too. Fortunately, not only was Barbara a good sailor but the North Atlantic was a lot calmer than on most of my destroyer days escorting convoys. I might add that in those immediate post-war years air travel for civilians, or Clydesdale horses, or pregnant women wasn't an option.

Sailing away from Scotland was, for me, a sad parting as I realized I was leaving for good. Oh, I might return for visits, but this was it—a new world, a new life, and as we throbbed our way down the beautiful Firth of Clyde toward the open ocean I was passing through the waters I had so often sailed. We sailed past Gourock, Hunter's Quay, Kirn (where as a boy I had helped old George with his boat rentals), Dunoon, the Cloch lighthouse, Innellan, Largs, Rothesay, the showpiece Isle of Arran, and finally round the Mull of Kintyre to the accompaniment of darkness and the slow up and down pitch of a ship moving into the long rollers of the North Atlantic.

My eyes became a little misty as those sights and memories passed slowly by. At moments, had I heard the sound of the bagpipes, tears would I'm sure have appeared. My thoughts were not just about myself but of the thousands of Scots who over decades, many under desperate circumstances, had emigrated to Nova Scotia, Newfoundland, Canada, Australia, New Zealand and America; some as children like John Muir who became the great American naturalist who virtually set up America's wondrous National Parks system.

I was lucky. Oh, certainly I was taking a chance, but I knew where I was going, had friends and support. This wasn't a voyage into the unknown as thousands before me faced.

After an 8-day crossing all arrived safely and without incident in New York, the Clydesdales included. Well, there were a couple of incidents, both surrounding one of our passengers, a union longshoreman and a labor organizer who seemed to have access to an unlimited amount of whisky. We were told an old dockside story that a couple of cases had broken open during shipment. This same labor organizer, familiar with ports around the world, offered to convey me and wife from ship to cab without visiting customs or officialdom in general. I politely declined. Through my father, who worked for a shipping company, I knew how politically powerful union longshoremen can be.

My wife's family welcomed us back joyously while at the same time preparing a welcome for their first grandchild. Fortunately, too, the house owned by my wife's grandfather, William Foster, long-term chairman of the Hingham selectmen, was large enough to provide us a small space of our own.

For me, however, there was but one thought uppermost: Find a job. Within days of arrival I was making appointments, sending out resumes, scouting advertisements.

My biggest problem was, did I want to break away from journalism? I was unsure, especially as an application to the *Boston Globe* had resulted only in encouragement, and the acceptance of two or three feature stories, but not a permanent job.

However, just as I was seriously considering a couple of nonwriting offers a friend of the family suggested I talk with Win Brooks, one of the top editors of William Randolph Hearst's then three Boston papers—the morning *Record*, the afternoon *American* and *The Sunday Advertiser*. Mr. Brooks who, from the outset, struck me more as a *New York Times* than a Hearst type editor, offered me a temporary job on the "lobster" (all-night) shift on the afternoon *American*. I gratefully accepted, and that impromptu decision, in fact, made my career choice for me. I would continue in journalism.

There was no faster way to pick up the American idiom, and Boston variants, than to work on a Hearst newspaper, either outside on the street, accompanying a photographer, covering fires, shootings, stabbings, accidents of all varieties, or inside on rewrite. I did both.

The afternoon *American* was produced on a wing and a prayer. Apart from foreign and national wire copy, local and New England news was covered by one night reporter, part time district correspondents and three, sometimes only two, rewrite men who basically updated local and New England stories from the then afternoon *Boston Globe*, backed up by a few phone calls.

I subbed for a time for one of those rewrite men who, I learned later was "indisposed" and who had had bouts of "indisposition" over many years.

Everyone, including the news and city editors and deskmen, was helpful. For example how else do you learn that Quincy's Fore River Bridge is spelled "Fore" not "Four."

What I learned on the street beat, riding with the night photographer, was a bit different. In Boston in 1947 blacks, called anything from "spades" to "jigaboos" in communication between radio cars and the city desk, were largely ignored. It took the very blunt charge of "racism" by Boston Celtic basketball star Bill Russell to awaken public concern. There were also religious animosities. I remember an Irish Catholic reporter telling me that he couldn't attend the wedding of a friend because it meant entering a Baptist church.

Let's face it, Boston physically in the post-war 1940s was a gray-looking shabby, parochial city, it's waterfront covered in coal dust and shuttered off from the city by rail lines, coal cars and old broken down wooden fences plastered with tattered playbills, political flyers and "keep out" signs. Many of its fine old historic buildings designed by Charles Bulfinch and Alexander Parris were hidden by signs, billboards and even false fronts.

The city had not yet shaken off the devastating criticism made by an article in *Fortune* magazine in 1933.

"The great families of Boston," it said, "did not go in for talent. They went in for power, for wealth, for acquisition, for control. And on the basis of comparison there can be no doubt but that the Bostonian of today has withdrawn from productive enterprise. He has lost the political control of his city. He is no longer a figure, as he was a dominant figure a hundred years ago in the government of the nation."

It went on: "He no longer leads either in public opinion or in private thought and he has so completely lost his leadership in the arts that his former influence has been a subject for satire."

The latter was a reference to Boston's decision to ban certain books and plays from being sold or acted in the city. Censorship had made the term, "banned in Boston," a national vaudeville joke.

This then was the inheritance the city gave those of us emerging from World War II, especially those born elsewhere. However, what had not deteriorated was Harvard University, the Massachusetts Institute of Technology and the city's great university hospitals, a fact that for a time seemed forgotten, like the beauty of Boston harbour and entire archipelago. And Boston's eleven newspapers had to spend so much effort simply staying alive and solvent that they avoided controversy and provided little leadership except for a few somewhat rarefied editorials such as some of the Globe's "Uncle Dudleys."

During my days, and nights, at the Hearst paper I kept in touch with the *Globe* which, despite still being known by some as the "housemaids' paper," struck me as the soundest of this over-newspapered town. Three *Globes*—morning, afternoon and Sunday; three Hearst papers—morning *Record*, afternoon *American* and *Sunday Advertiser*; three *Heralds*—morning *Herald*, afternoon *Traveler* and *Sunday Herald*, and finally the morning *Boston Post* and the *Christian Science Monitor*. Gradually they died, merged or consolidated.

My contact at the *Globe* was city editor Charlie Merrill, a Harvard and Hingham man, who knew my wife's family (thank God for networking) which led to an invitation to meet with *Globe* editor, Laurence L. Winship, also a Harvard man (like the entire upper echelon) with a quite formidable editorial reputation and taciturn demeanor. I guess I passed muster and Mr. Merrill offered me a temporary position when my stint with the *Hearst American* finished, which it did a month later. So my sole challenge was to do a good enough job to become a permanent employee.

Evidently I met the challenge as I was still at the *Globe* 37 years later having served in successive years as reporter, rewrite man, deskman, and as medical-education-science writer, financial-business editor, managing editor, columnist and associate editor. And I had no reason to leave except the *Globe* quite suddenly decided to enforce mandatory retirement for executives at age 65.

It was 1985 and I was about to be 65 but more to the point, the new retirement policy embraced the *Globe*'s then personable hot shot "how the hell are you," editor Tom Winship, son of retiring editor Laurence Winship.

Tom never publicly criticized the new policy but I knew personally that he felt blindsided by the move and warned me one day that he was "having the devil of a time" finding an appropriate transitional position and urging me to step up my own search.

I felt I was luckier than Tom who eventually received a special fellowship from the Gannett newspaper group in New York whereas I was invited to join the then newly formed McCormack Institute of Public Affairs at UMass Boston—virtually across the street from *The Boston Globe* on Morrissey Boulevard.

I gladly accepted the invitation from the Institute's director Professor Edmund Beard, and, as a Senior Fellow, spent the next 10 years teaching, lecturing and running conferences on urban affairs at the Institute.

Furthermore, I was able to continue to write my column (though not for the *Globe* which ostensibly banned retiree columns) but for the *Patriot Ledger* of Quincy at the invitation of the *Ledger*'s then most respected editor, William "Bill" Ketter.

This perfect arrangement, leastwise for me, lasted until I chose my own retirement in 1995, age 75.

No one will admit why the *Globe* rather suddenly decided to enforce mandatory retirement for executives at 65, but it conveniently cleared the way for William O. "Bill" Taylor to choose his own editorial leaders after taking over as publisher from his father, Davis, in 1978. It was known, however, that while Bill and

Tom Winship respected each other, their socio-political views often differed.

So in 1984 and in line with the new retirement policy, Tom Winship retired, and Bill Taylor appointed Michael Janeway, managing editor of the *Sunday Globe,* to replace him as editor.

Janeway, a tall taciturn type with a somewhat superior but tactless style, was less than popular in the city room, a complete opposite from Winship. What happened was inevitable. Within 18 months he resigned. It was not Bill Taylor's finest hour, though that was about to come.

I will say more about my 37 years in the *Globe* in a later book; about its characters, egos and jealousies and its rise to fame to become worth $1.1 billion, the price the *New York Times* paid to buy it in 1993—the most money every paid to buy a single newspaper.

For now, however, I would close my war years, by saying how they nurtured my two desires—a love of the sea and ships and a career in journalism. Although to do one I had to volunteer for the Royal Navy and to do the other change countries.

Through it all, at least toward the end, there had to be one constant and that constant was the small-town of Hingham where my most memorable ship was built—a ship which played a fighting role on D-day (before and beyond)—and the town where I met my wife, raised a family and commuted to a most satisfying 37 years at the *Boston Globe* and 10 more at the University of Massachusetts.

What's more, the bustling war-time shipyard where 23,000 people worked night and day for three years is now a high-end development of water-view luxury homes, apartments and modern stores and restaurants. More than that, the shipyard which under lend-lease built and turned over 40 destroyer escorts to the Royal Navy, did something quite unexpected. It has named one of its new streets – *H.M.S. Stayner* Drive, a thoughtful memorial.

—End—

THE SINKING OF THE *EMPRESS OF CANADA*

Freda Bonner, one of six chief petty officer WRENS (Women's Royal Naval Service) was aboard the troop ship Empress of Canada when she was torpedoed and sunk by an Italian submarine off West Africa in March, 1943.

There were some 30 women aboard as well as approximately 1,900 men. Numbers vary, especially of those rescued, as three ships took part in the rescue at different times. Also the majority of those aboard, including 300 Italian POWs, spoke little English which explains why so little has ever been written about this tragic sinking.

The author was a Lieutenant aboard the first rescue ship, H.M.S. Boreas, to reach survivors who had already spent two days in lifeboats, floats and in some cases in the water hanging on to debris.

The author's assignment was to find space for the survivors—space on a destroyer is limited. The women were sheltered in the wardroom, given water and soap to wash off sticky oil and on their own initiative, rummaged around our cabins for clean clothing.

The author spoke briefly to some of the women but in the bedlam of Polish, Czech and French languages, picked up no particular names.

Then, some 17 years later, he met one of them, Freda Bonner who had come to Boston to take a master's degree at the Harvard School of Public Health. There, Bonner met a Boston Globe reporter, who, on hearing of her rescue by H.M.S. Boreas, *linked Bonner to one of her Globe colleagues, the author, and brought us together... again.*

So what follows is Freda Bonner's first-person story of the sinking of the Empress of Canada *and the rescue of survivors.*

On March 2, 1943 the *Empress of Canada* sailed from Durban, South Africa bound for the United Kingdom. On board were six CPO WRENSs, W/T, Betty Dart, Margaret Finch, Lilly Feeney, Pam Gray, Betty Leitch and Freda Bonner, part of the first contingent of WRENS ever to leave the United Kingdom. At the fall of Singapore they had been evacuated to Colombo. After the attempted air-borne invasion of Colombo, they sailed in an armed merchant cruiser with the Far Eastern Fleet under command of Admiral Somerville in the *Warspite* to Mombasa. Now, having been overseas for over two years, they were going home on leave.

Also on board were about 30 naval officers and 60 ratings, some RAF personnel, 300 Italian prisoners of war in charge of an Italian officer, who was on parole, and about 200 French, Greek and Polish refugees, including 10 women. All the naval officers were returning home on long overdue leave, some had been overseas for over four years.

Early in 1943, our shipping losses, due to sinkings by submarines, had been formidable, therefore, only service personnel or those with special reasons were given passage. However, the ship, the *Empress of Canada,* one of the largest passenger ships in the world, could sail at 28 knots which was considered to be almost too fast to be hit by a torpedo. Owing to her speed, she sailed unescorted.

Our course took us far into the middle of the South Atlantic.

We never sighted another ship. Our ship was half empty; the days passed uneventfully. Everybody was in good spirits and looking forward to leave. Three days after sailing, a 17-year old Greek girl stowaway was found. She was married to an RAF sergeant on board.

Our first port of call was to be Takoradi on the Gold Coast where we were to pick up a VIP. However, on March 11th a signal was received from Admiralty telling us to alter our course for Freetown.

March 12th, 1943, was a beautiful day, we were on the equator. During that day our, speed had obviously increased and we were zigzagging. As the day went by we saw overturned lifeboats and other wreckage of recent disasters; however, I do not think that any one was much concerned about it as we had absolute confidence that our ship was so fast nothing could touch her.

The late Lt. Cmdr. Kenneth Forman and I were sitting on deck. He remarked that "nothing ever happened to him." He was one of the very few Japanese interpreters. He had been flown out of Hong Kong and also out of Singapore before everybody else. For the last year he had been at Mombasa and again he was to have flown home. However, as he was getting on board the plane, it was found that he had not had his yellow fever inoculation, so he was not allowed to fly. In fact, he caught a cruiser, sailed a day ahead of schedule from Mombasa to Durban thus permitting him to catch the *Empress of Canada*. He had not been home for six years.

That evening passed as usual except that the ship was vibrating noisily and obviously her engines were going flat out. "Lights out" on troopships is at 11:00 p.m. we were all in our cabins by about 10:30 PM.

Shortly after 11 PM we heard a dull thud, far, far below us. We knew at once that we had been torpedoed and within a few minutes the ship stopped dead. No alarms sounded. There were no lights. Even the emergency system failed. A brilliant or freak shot had hit us amidships in the engine room. At first there was an uncanny silence and then we heard urgent footsteps on the stairs.

We WRENs were all in one cabin and immediately we had our coats and life jackets on. I put my hand into my dressing case to pick up some money but immediately I thought, "I shall never need this again," so left it and, instead, picked up a packet of cigarettes. Why? I do not smoke.

In a very few minutes we were ready and joined the stream of crew and passengers all making their way urgently to the upper decks. It was pitch dark. Everybody was silent but urgent footsteps were everywhere. We now knew that another torpedo could not miss. We were a "sitting bird."

It took us a seemingly long time to reach the upper deck; the great majority had arrived ahead of us. When we arrived at our boat station we found only one person waiting for us, Lt. Cmdr. Forman who had given up his place in another boat in order to help us. Our boat was overturned in the water.

There was a moon and therefore we had some light. The ship had stopped dead and heeled over with the decks at a sharp angle. Every where the Royal Naval Officers had taken charge. Some were throwing rafts and floats into the sea, others were letting down ropes. Up forward Surgeon Lt. Jacklyn was getting refugees into the only remaining boat alongside. Other naval officers in charge of boats waited until they were filled to maximum capacity before pulling off. Owing to the sharp angle of the ship, over half the lifeboats either could not be launched or had overturned. One naval officer saw that the Italian POWs got off the ship; they all jumped into the sea.

As the *Empress* was not sinking we thought the ship was safer than the sea. However, the submarine Captain was honoring the Geneva Convention, which states that when a ship is mortally

Barbara H. Menzies.

"800 Survivors were rescued from the *Empress of Canada.*"

5.

stricken, the passengers and crew should be allowed 20 minutes to abandon ship.

We were not left in doubt much longer; soon the ship was torpedoed again. There was now no time to be lost and everybody left on board got off as quickly as possible.

They jumped, climbed down on rope ladders and slid down the ropes. Many who hastily slid down the ropes suffered rope burns which, unfortunately was later to cost them their lives for they were unable to cling to the sides of the rafts and floats.

As soon as we were off the *Empress*, it was imperative to get a good distance from her to avoid being sucked under when she finally sank, stern first.

As we were all pushing away from the *Empress*, suddenly and directly in front of us, the seas opened and a huge black monster came up from the deep. It was the submarine. At gun point the Captain ordered the nearest life boat to come alongside. This boat was in charge of Cmdr. Dick Thatcher and by chance in his boat was the one Italian officer. He made himself known and he was taken off. He did a kind of "Highland Fling" of joy on the conning tower of the submarine. The submarine cruised amongst us slowly, took photographs, did us no harm and then dived under. Shortly afterwards she fired a final salvo of torpedoes and again hit the *Empress*.

It was about two hours later that the *Empress* suddenly upended and with a dreadful, awful roaring noise plunged into the depths of the sea. This dreadful awful roar remained with me night after night for nearly a year.

It was a long night. There were many cries for help. At long last the dawn came. All around us were rafts with red sails, boats with red sails, there were Carley floats and there were still many in the sea who were alive and calling for help. Lifebelts had supported them all through the night. Also among us could be seen the fins of sharks and barracudas. Gradually, all those in the sea found room in the boats and the cries for help gradually ceased.

We were on the Equator, 700 miles from Cape Palmas, an SOS has been sent and the position had been given. There was hope that if we did not drift too far away from the present position we might expect to be rescued.

We drifted, but not Surgeon Lt. Jacklyn who for two days swam from raft to raft and float to float, rendering help to the injured until finally he was lost. He was awarded a posthumous Mention in Despatches. I saw Commander Puxley, and two other naval officers getting off an overcrowded raft that was in danger of sinking, they got onto the top of an overturned lifeboat. They were never seen again. Cmdr. Puxley had been married for a short time before going overseas three years previously. He had never seen the home his bride had prepared for him.

On the second afternoon a Sunderland Flying Boat flew over us, we knew then that rescue was on the way. On the third evening as the sun was setting we saw the destroyer *H.M.S Boreas*. We watched her stopping over and over again to pick up survivors off the rafts and floats and soon it was our turn. There were rope nets down the sides of the destroyer. A soon as she stopped, sailors climbed down the sides and gathered up survivors on their shoulders, climbed up the ropes again with their burdens and handed them over to willing hands on deck and quickly returned for more. Every stop the Captain made to pick up survivors endangered his ship, for there was a very real possibility that the submarine was still in the vicinity and eager for more victims.

Actually, to rescue us the *Boreas* had sailed all the way from close to Gibraltar at top speed. The following day a frigate also arrived. *Boreas* picked up about 700 survivors. The officers and crew gave up their cabins, gave us clothing, food and drink; their many kindnesses are unforgettable.

Two days later we were landed at Freetown and there we waited for the frigate to bring in the remaining survivors. It was a sad accounting. ALL six WRENs and 10 women refugees had been saved but the cost had been high. Over 700 had been lost. These losses would have been much higher if it had not been for the Royal Naval Officers who gave their lives "doing their duty." During those days, while awaiting rescue, many were the thoughts that passed through our minds and many were the promises made of "what we would do if we were rescued." I wonder, "did we keep our promises?"

Four years later I was sitting in a garden in Vancouver, Canada, and uncertain as to what I should do. Suddenly, I knew that I must be a doctor. Was it the memory of the naval doctor, Surgeon Lieutenant Jacklyn swimming from raft to raft that led me to make this decision? I believe it was.

Finally the *Mauretania* brought us to England. From there I had to get to my home in Dublin. By accident the porter at Euston put me in the wrong train. After three changes, an Inspector told me that I must change again at Bangor. I was tired, exhausted and in tones of despair asked "Must I change yet again?"

A woman beside me arrogantly remarked "You're lucky to be travelling! Don't you know there is a war on?"

A rather macabre postscript to the story came when we were given our first sit down meal at Freetown. The main course was barracuda.

Ian Menzies asked his friend Commander John Hall, who had commanded HMS Stayner, to write an earlier account of a convoy that set out for Murmansk in 1942. Commander Hall, as a favor to his executive officer on Stayner, dictated this account and presented the audio tape, along with good wishes, to Ian and Barbara Menzies upon their 45th wedding anniversary in June 1990.

This fateful convoy (PQ17) set sail from Iceland in June 1942. Of the 32 ships in the convoy, mostly American, 23 were lost or abandoned. John Hall was the captain of one of the escorting ships, HMS Lotus, a corvette. This story of that tragic voyage is told not only in the voice of a naval officer and professional sailor, but in the voice of a rescuing humanitarian.

The account has been transcribed and considerably edited. Names of people, places and ships have been checked for spellings where possible, or otherwise noted as (sic) by Marla Menzies.

John Hall's Account of PQ 17
The Convoy to Murmansk

When I got home from a post in East Africa, the Navy put me in command of a corvette. In Edinburgh, Robbs were building a ship called *Lotus*, and I went to Edinburgh and took command.

We finally got *Lotus* ready and did our trials, and then we were sent round to the famous "Monkey" Stevenson to be worked up at Tobermory. It was my first visit to "Monkey" (nick-named for his agility), although I was to go again later, of course, in *Stayner*. Then we went down to Londonderry, which was a very nice little port.

She (*Lotus*) was painted the North Atlantic convoy camouflage —white and pale blue and pale pink. The principle was to paint up the dark parts and paint down the lighter parts, and she looked very pretty. The camouflage must have been effective as they kept it right up throughout the war.

This is really where the Convoy story starts:

I was sitting in a very old carriage rumbling along between Belfast and Londonderry, and I looked out the window as we approached Londonderry, hoping to spot my ship. I couldn't find her at first. Then I saw her. And she was a different colour! To my astonishment she was painted dark gray, light gray, and black. I thought that was very odd, so when I got on board, I said to number one, "What's the new colour for?

"Oh," he said, "we're going to Russia."

And that's the first I knew about a Russian convoy. I was told that this convoy was Number PQ 17 and that we would be sailing in 10 days' time. They stocked us up with this, that, and the other—and I must say my officers did a first class job loading it—and before we got home, we were very grateful they had done so.

Down the River Foyle we started, and as we went alongside the oiler, I got a signal. I read it and I thought, " Heavens this is not me, surely."

It said: "To *Lotus* from C and C Western Approaches. Take under your command the following corvettes: *Lotus, Dianella, Starwort* and *Poppy* and proceed to Iceland to the Port of Seydisfjordur and place yourself under the command of Commander Broome, who is the Senior Officer of the escort for convoy PQ 17."

Well, you can imagine what that did with my hope that I was going to be able to tag along and become experienced in this war. But as everybody knows, when war comes, one moves fast in experience and in stature. And really, I felt very much humbled to be in charge of this, but of course I'd been a permanent RNR Officer and I held quite a lot of rank stowed away in my kit bag; nearly all the others were RNVR Officers. And away we went.

It was June 1942—a lovely summer—and as we sailed up through the Western Isles, the world really looked very peaceful indeed. The only disruption was when we got clear of the north of Scotland where we came across an awful lot of floating mines, and I got my first smack-down from the commanding officer of one of the corvettes. I thought it would be a good idea to give the boys a little gunnery practice and from the next ship down—and very smartly—the word came: "Wouldn't waste the ammunition. We might need it and those mines are quite safe."

So on we went. The thing that struck me most, was the change in the climate. I had been north before, but most of my life had been spent in the tropics, and it's quite certain the light and the atmosphere up in the north are different. As we went north towards Seydisfjordur, I was struck by the atmospheric and light changes and how different they were from further south. By the time we arrived at Seydisfjordur the sun didn't set at all.

Arrival at Seydisfjordur was quite spectacular—a harbour surrounded by high mountains, the tops of which were covered in ice and snow and gushing rivers roared down the snowy mountain. I watched these with great interest through my binoculars, wondering what sort of fish the waters might hold as I'd been a fisherman all my life.

The sun still shone, and there were many, many, ships there. *Keppel* was there—the senior officer's ship—Jackie Broome's destroyer. There were some old 4-stacker jobs, our corvettes, 4 trawlers, and goodness knows how many ships. I've forgotten how many ships there were in the escort. The convoy was not there because it was being mustered in Hvalfjord on the other side of Iceland.

The convoy was to consist of some 35 merchant ships with incredible numbers of tanks and aircraft and things in their cargo. The value was estimated at something astronomical and would be sufficient to support an army of 50,000 men if it all got to

Russia. Of course, it didn't. And this is part of the story of PQ 17.

We arrived in Iceland just before the end of June, and on the 29th of June the convoy sailed from Hvalfjord. It was a very long convoy, and it took 22 days for us to arrive at the destination. We were all just about dead beat by the time that happened. It was a sorry number of ships that we actually got in, in the end, sometime just before the end of July.

We lost 2 ships straightaway in the fog. One went aground, and she gave a disastrous SOS signal which possibly indicated to the enemy that some activity was starting. It was unfortunate, but in the end, didn't make a great deal of difference because the Germans were well ready for this convoy to be run, and they mustered a lot of forces to stop it from ever getting to Russia. A major unit headed by the battleship *Tirpitz* were waiting in northern ports in Norway to sail and to intercept this convoy. In reply we had large forces also in the area but they were not to be risked beyond a certain point.

It was hoped that we would trap any big force, if we could, and bring it to action. In fact, I remember Admiral Burnett (sic), who was in charge of the cruiser squadron, giving us a talk before we went.

"We are the cheese in the trap," he said.

Sadly, I'm afraid, it didn't come off. We sat there in fine weather, waiting for our turn to leave, and we left on the 30th. There was a little fog here and there as we steamed north. The weather was still fine, a little fog, but nothing very much, and then we found our convoy and spread out. The convoy was now reduced to 33 ships—merchant ships, in columns of 4, were hidden in the convoy.

The escort was really quite imposing. Two ex-banana boats— the *Palomares* and the *Pozerica*—had been converted to flagships; they were just bristling with guns, and they were in the middle of the convoy. They had no anti-submarine equipment at all. Apart from them, we had 3 fleet destroyers—*Keppel*, with Jackie Broome in command of the whole outfit, and *Offa*, and *Fury*, one on either side of the convoy. Then 3 ex-US 4-stacker job destroyers—*Ledbury*, *Wilton*, and *Leamington*; 4 corvettes—*Lotus*, *Poppy*, *La Malouine*, and *Dianella*—these were the 4 corvettes that I had brought up. We had, as well, 4 old Smokey Joe trawlers—*Lord Austin*, *Lord Middleton*, *Northern Gem*, and *Ayershire*, (skippered by a very colourful character who eventually became Sir Leo Gradville the senior judge of the metropolitan area of London; he caused quite a lot of stir). We also had 2 rescue ships—one British and one Russian. We had 2 submarines in case there was an opportunity to get a good shot at the German big ships, which we didn't and the subs went back.

That was the quite imposing escort that we had as we stooged along. We were given areas of influence in which we could move around rather than fixed positions, out of which we were not supposed to move without direct orders from *Keppel*. *Lotus* was on the port bow of the convoy, *Poppy*, our opposite number on the starboard bow, *La Malouine* on the port quarter and *Dianella* on the starboard quarter. When we joined the convoy, it was on a course of 045 heading up north of Bear Island. A little later the next day we had Jan Mayen Island on our port beam. We were due to go into Murmansk the next day and part of the escort would have broken off by then.

Unfortunately, before we ever got to that point, the Germans caused such havoc by bombing and strafing Murmansk that it was quite impossible to put a ship in there, so the whole lot of us were sent on to Archangel.

The weather was quite extraordinary. As you got further north the light seemed to change. Going north with the all-day and all-night sun was incredible, but the Arctic can be very quick to change its coat. However, the weather was lovely; we steamed along silently and nothing happened. For a while.

The Germans picked us up by a Dornier flying boat, flying a reconnaissance from the north of Norway right to the ice cap and back again. She continued to trail us. She was just a sitting duck on the horizon that somebody occasionally had a pop at. She was so low down, she used to go round and round and every so often she'd be relieved by another Dornier; the two of them would go round and round and then the other one would leave.

There were little patches of humour here and there. Somebody made a cheeky signal to the Dornier one day, saying: "Please go round the other way you're making me dizzy."

And the reply came back immediately: "Anything to oblige a bloody Britisher."

And they turned round and went the other way.

So we stooged along and wondered what was going to happen next.

On the first of July 1942 things started to happen, and from then on we had attacks from the air. All the attacks were from F 115s—a German torpedo-carrying aircraft. I can't really remember how many attacks we had, but we didn't really lose any ships because fire-power from the convoy was terrific. We knew, also, that over the horizon the home fleet force and the cruisers were not more than about 10 or 15 miles away.

Then, on the 1st of July as we were abeam of Jan Mayen Island, we were attacked. Whether the first attacks were just feelers to see what the opposition was going to be like, I don't know, but they didn't do us any serious damage. On July the 2nd, though, we lost one ship, and there was also evidence of submarines lying in a line. Since it was daylight all the time, they were seen from time to time but they didn't seem to manage an attack.

There were sporadic attacks from time to time, but nothing very serious happened until the 4th. That was the big day.

We'd had one incident of a pilot coming down after he'd been damaged and actually landing on the water. We watched a very brave action by his colleague who went down and landed in full fire from all the convoy and picked him up. The pilot rowed across in a rubber dinghy and left his plane floating. It floated right by us. Everybody really felt this was a terrific job done by the chap who rescued his mate.

Then, on the radar screen we had information that an attack was developing from the southeast. I don't know how many of these aircraft there were, but they appeared like a swarm of bees flying very low towards us just over the horizon. The ships opened up, fire started and only a few of these aircraft pressed home the attack. The leader lost his life because he flew right over the convoy—absolutely straight—headed straight for a ship. He came down, dropped his torpedo, and when he was absolutely ablaze, went out and ditched on the side. We discovered afterward from German sources, that he was the leader; his name was Heineman (sic). I think he really did a wonderful job. Another one who came after him, also came through the convoy and he ditched too. Whether he was saved, I'm not sure. A number of other aircraft, I think most certainly, never got home, and the majority of these dropped their torpedoes outside the range of our guns and turned to port and away back. They didn't face the barrage of fire which was absolutely terrific. I think a number of these were hit, but their torpedoes did us no damage.

We lost, in that big attack, 2 ships—the *Hooper* and a Russian merchant ship, the *Azurbaijan*. She was damaged but she got underway again. The story was that the crew took to the boats and the chief officer ordered them back on board with a hand machine gun and fired on them until they did come back. The officer was a woman, which we were to learn later of course—in Russia, women were doing everything.

That was a tremendous night, the evening of the 4th of July. In the morning we'd had the sight of the American ship—the *Wainwright*, I think—and she broke out into flags over all for the

4th of July. Other American ships with the home fleet came and disappeared; withdrawn and sent back, I think.

The attack left us somewhat short. One ship was badly blown up; her boiler was hit and she sank very quickly. The rescue ships picked up the pieces at the back of the convoy, and on we stooged.

It was 8 o'clock when this attack took place, and the menace from the big ships of the German fleet which had been gradually moving up from Norway, was getting worse. Although Jackie Broome was perfectly prepared to go on and thought we were doing extremely well under the circumstances, we got the signal that the convoy was to scatter! Well you know scattering convoys is all right if you've got a whole, big ocean all the way around, but when you've got ice to port and enemy to starboard and nothing very much ahead or behind you, it's a bit problematical.

Anyway, the convoy was told to scatter, and at the same time a signal was made to Broome saying the destroyers escorting PQ 17 were to return at high speed and join the home fleet.

Now, there was a terrible controversy over this—in fact, there was a law case in which Jackie Broome sued somebody for saying in a book that he ran away. Jackie won the case and stung the chap who wrote it for damages of forty thousand pounds, but that of course was a much later story.

The idea in everybody's mind was that these destroyers were being withdrawn to make a submarine torpedo attack, probably on the *Tirpitz* which was known to be in northern waters.

It was a question, really, of how far east one could get until they, the German surface force, were out of safe cover. And that's perhaps why the convoy was told to scatter. We went in a fan-out from the forward and silence reigned. For some time there were ships all over the horizon as they all went different speeds.

What was the escort to do? Well, the trawlers got together in a huddle and stooged along and collected one or two slower ships.

The 4 corvettes—*Poppy, La Malouine, Lotus,* and *Dianella*—were grabbed immediately by the two flagships. As Jackie Broom had left, we had no senior officer of the escort. In fact, I was fast becoming the most senior of the escorting skippers. We were told to screen *Pozerica* and *Palomares* because they had no defense against submarines. It seemed sensible at the time and I suppose it was. So I placed the 4 corvettes around these 2 ships and we stooged on. We'd been going possibly a day and a half—as there was no night, it's very difficult to remember the sequence of events

After we'd been going a day or so, the SOS signals started up. The German submarines had got themselves organized and started torpedoing these ships one at a time. They'd all headed away from the convoy and were to approach Archangel by turning south, but the ones that turned north got onto the ice field. *Pankraft* was one of those way up on the ice field, and she was making a very loud SOS signal, which could be heard from the loud speakers. She was screaming for help, said she had been bombed and had abandoned ship. Then all the ships were opening up with SOS signals. Dozens of them it seemed, between us and the North Pole.

Palomares and *Pozerica* were intended to make to the eastern side in the Matochkin Strait. There are two islands off North Russia with the same shapes as New Zealand—and the name is the same too—Novaye Zemlya. Matochkin Strait runs between them. I knew they were going there, and when *Pankraft* made her signal, I measured up the distance and found she was 30 or 40 miles behind us on the ice edge. So I made the signal to *Palomares* and said: "Request permission to return to assist *Pankraft.*"

I learned afterwards, there was a signal to say that the *Tirpitz* and other craft were reported heading northeast across the sea and that escorts should make best speed to the eastwards, to try and preserve themselves, and to pick up survivors after the battle which would ensue.

It was fortunate for me, I didn't know that. And we went back and left the other 3 corvettes screening *Palomares* and *Pozerica*.

When I found the ship, my inclination was to sink her instead of leaving her there. But the moment I made a shot at her, the people in the lifeboats screamed at me that the thing was full of explosives, and that she'd blow us all to pieces if I hit her. So we picked up the lot—and it was some 4 or 5 hours later by the time we got them on board—and we turned to head east again. I headed for Matochkin Strait, as it seemed reasonable to go in there until the heavy ships of the enemy turned for home.

We were headed for Matochkin Strait when, about 12 hours later, we saw a yellow flare on the starboard horizon, obviously survivors from some ship, so we headed for them. I was conscious of lots of submarines around, but when we got there we found there were 3 boats and 2 rafts. Now we had something like 150 men from *Pankraft* on board by this time, but I couldn't find the submarine that had torpedoed this lot. So we picked up the survivors and—extraordinarily—Commodore Dowding was among them. His ship, *River Afton*, had been hit. Dowding, stayed on board my ship until we got into Archangel.

"Thank God for this [immersion] suit!" he said, as he came aboard. "It saved my bloody life today!"

By this time *Lotus* had over 200 men on board, which made quite a crowd on a little corvette.

We'd been on the ice for some time, but when we thought it would be reasonably safe, we decided to cut across the corner and go down to Matochkin Strait. As a sailor, I found it extraordinary to be in uncharted waters, and going into Matochkin Strait, I had no chart to show me the way in. But the next morning, when we arrived off at Matochkin Strait, to my delight, I found there was a lead light when we rounded the buoy.

On the point just inside, we found *Pozerica, Palomares*, and 3 fleet mine sweepers, which were taking passage with this convoy and heading for duty in Archangel. There were 3 or 4 merchant ships as well, and the 3 corvettes that I'd left behind.

All the passengers I had on board were up on deck, and as we approached *Palomares*, that ship's crew cheered the *Lotus*. It was quite embarrassing, really. I didn't think of myself as having a charmed life, but they seemed to think I had and were congratulating me on our return to safety.

We went alongside *Pozerica* and had a little conference with Captain Lawford.

"Let's go over and see the ship on the other side," he said. "And see if she will take your passengers."

This merchant ship very willingly took my 200 passengers off, and after a little discussion, it was decided Jack Dowding, the Commodore, would stay with me.

We could count about 5 merchant ships now that were either in this inlet or along the coast. In fact, there was one ship that had parked itself along this inlet on Novaya Zemlya, gone ashore and set up camp, having nudged their ship onto the beach. Quite incredible. But we thought that there was enough to form a little convoy. Lawford, who was the senior captain, decided we should get out quickly, because the moment the Germans discovered that we were taking shelter in Matochkin Strait, we could be strafed, So a convoy was organized.

One ship was known to have gone half way through and into the Kara Sea. I was told to go and fetch her out. Once again there didn't seem to be any lead lights through the Strait. These were spectacular islands with great mountains on either side and the passage between was quite narrow. It tested the difference between the amateur yachtsman and the professional sailor, and I was not at all anxious to chance my arm on taking the ship through this narrow, windy passage to find the ship on the inside. So I talked to Hoppy Newton, my gunnery officer, who still lives in the

Channel Islands and who had been a yachtsman there before the war.

"What do we do?" I asked him. "How do we navigate this?"

"Oh, keep to the steep side and away from the shallow," he said.

So out of one's ken as a professional navigator, to have such methods, but it was a word of wisdom. So we steamed through and found the ship in the middle, and the first thing she said was: "Don't try to anchor."

Apparently Matochkin Strait was like a crack in the earth's surface. It was sharp like a 'V' that went down, god knows how far, and it was extremely difficult to get an anchor to stay; it bumble-bumble-bumbled, down into the crack. Anyway, we weren't for anchoring, and we got her underway and brought her out to the western harbour at the entrance place.

When we got underway and steamed out of Novaya Zemlya, we must have had about 8 or 9 merchant ships, the mine sweepers, the corvettes and in the *Lotus*, the commodore of the whole outfit, Captain Dowding.

The moment we'd got outside, we sent out another ship to try and collect other carriers that were hiding in the inlets in the Novaya Zemlya coast. This produced another 3 or so, but I'm afraid we left the one that had put her nose on the beach and set up camp.

As we stooged on down, the weather was brilliant, but you could run into a fog that was just like opening a door and going through into somewhere else, and we lost one ship. Lost in the fog, she turned back into Matochkin Strait.

We went close in down the coast of Novaya Zemlya towards Archangel, and we picked up refugees in lifeboats and survivors from various ships on the way. One incredible save was the captain of one of the ships, whom we found just floating in the water. Why he was alone, I don't know. He had a jolly good life jacket.

Incredibly, he was still alive, because the water was cold—damn cold and filled with ice—even though the weather was fine.

We got to the south end of Nova Zemlya. There were a few submarine attacks on the way, but we were able to cope with these because we had enough escorts to form a formidable anti-submarine force. We ran into ice before we got to the entrance of the Dvina River and had to make it through this with the fog over the top of it. Finally we got out the other side and were heading down for a place in North Russia called Iokanka, but they shooshed us out of there quickly; they said they couldn't afford to have an air attack on their only northern port that was left except for Archangel.

Once outside, we got a really heavy and sustained air bombing attack—a high level bombing attack. I think by this time they'd assessed that the only two ships that really had anti-aircraft guns were the *Palomares* and *Pozerica*, Most of the others had either pom-pom or small arms. So, they dive bombed us and whizzed out of range before we could get at them. We lost one ship, and had a lot of near misses. Because the corvettes were highly maneuverable, one could stand up and look at these aircraft and the moment they were committed to their dive, could alter course. And we'd do it violently and put on speed. Although we had misses—near enough to wet everybody on deck—we weren't actually damaged at all.

Finally, a couple of days later—22 days from starting this convoy we arrived at the entrance to the Dvina River. *Poppy*, and myself in *Lotus*, were told to sweep the channel in. Since there might be mines, we were fitted with this tail, a magnetic mine clearance. So *Poppy* and I set up as a mine sweeping unit and swept the others into the Dvina River and arrived at Archangel.

I think I am right in saying we got 11 ships in. Sounds terrible, doesn't it? Very sad, the loss of this enormous quantity of equipment. As far as we, the escort, were concerned—and thinking about it much later—I came to the conclusion we'd done quite a good job when the figures for the actual loss of human beings in that entire convoy was around 200. Of course, the main purpose of convoy work is the safe arrival of your convoy. All in all, we felt very sad about that outcome.

What happened after that, of course, is another story altogether. We didn't get back until it became dark, and it was dark all night. We worked for the Russians from time to time.

We did several convoys to Murmansk and other places. The weather could change in half an hour. You could go from reasonable, fine weather to Force 9 gale in one direction and to Force 9 in the other direction in about 2 hours. It really was quite incredible. I can remember on one occasion, we lost a ship completely; she broke up—broke in half—and the destroyers that were with us in that convoy couldn't even turn around.

Anyway, there you are Ian, a badly told story of a convoy to North Russia, with very little about what the convoy was about. But I would recommend anyone who wants to know about the convoy to read a book called *The Destruction of PQ 17*, by David Irving. I've got it here and I can only read big print nowadays. It's a very good definitive account of the convoy. There are about 4 or 5 other books written by various people, most of them propaganda, because there was a lot of hate about it.

I will never be a broadcaster, Ian, but you asked me to do this so I thought I'd have a go.

John Hall and Kitty Hall visiting Ian and Barbara Menzies, in front of the Eastham, MA Coast Guard Station, fall 1980.

Printed in Great Britain
by Amazon